Where the Black Fish Swims

An Eskimo family's journey for survival
to escape the Spanish Flu in Alaska

Molly Hootch Hymes

8370 Eleusis Drive, Anchorage, Alaska 99502-4630
books@publicationconsultants.com—www.publicationconsultants.com

ISBN Number: 978-1-63747-150-0
eBook ISBN Number: 978-1-63747-152-4

Library of Congress Number: 2025947987

Copyright © 2025 Molly Hootch Hymes
—First Edition—

All rights reserved, including the right of reproduction in any form, or by any mechanical or electronic means including photocopying or recording, or by any information storage or retrieval system, in whole or in part in any form, and in any case not without the written permission of the author.

Manufactured in the United States of America

Dedication

I dedicate this book to the memory of Veronica Hootch Barrett. She was my aunt who told me about the life of my grandpa, Charlie Hootch, before he settled in Emmonak, Alaska. Her remembrance of my grandpa's early life and his journey to Emmonak became the source of this book. It was a story that I felt should be told, as it represents the lineage of my family and the village of my birth. My aunt Veronica passed away as I wrote the final chapter of this book on August 5, 2025.

Acknowledgment

This book would not have been possible without the encouragement of my husband, Alvin Hymes. It took the combined efforts of both of us to make it possible.

Chapter 1

I am Qataruaq, son of Unozroak, a Yupik, and I live in the village of Kagemuit on the banks of the Kusquqvak River in the territory of Alaska.

It is spring and the Kusquqvak River has flooded its banks. My family and I have taken shelter in the village BIA school, as our cabins have also flooded. The school is built on pilings, making it a safe building above the floodwaters. School has finished for the summer, and all the teachers have left for their homes outside the village.

The entire village has taken refuge in the school building. The village of Kagemuit is home to my family: grandpa and grandma, my two uncles and aunt, along with their children. It makes for a crowded situation, but we are always one big family that stays together to get through any crisis we encounter.

It has already been several days since we entered the school, and my patience is growing short. I am ready for the water to recede so we can get back to our cabin and prepare for fishing season. The one thing that makes being confined in the school building tolerable is the opportunity to go to the school kitchen and eat anything that doesn't require a can opener. My favorite item is peanut butter and jelly on the large Sailor Boy brand pilot crackers we could not afford to buy.

Each family brought dried fish, fresh fish, and waterfowl we caught before the floodwater came. We all shared the food. Soup was especially everyone's favorite. We brought soup made from ptarmigan, swan, geese, and fish, as soup serves many people. We drank a lot of Labrador tea while the elders drank coffee. With the availability of the school kitchen, fresh bread is baked or fried and has become another favorite.

The food from the school kitchen was left from the school season, which ended before the flood came. Everyone knew the flood was coming, so the school's supply of canned food was left for just this time, as the adults saw fit.

The school only taught classes to the sixth grade. All the students were my Pa's brother's and sister's children. Again, we were a big family even while in school. There were three teachers who divided their teaching between the diverse ages of students. One of the teachers also doubled as a nurse for the entire village. It was a blessing to have a village nurse, as it was a day's journey by kayak to an actual doctor's office.

I finished my school experience three years ago. The most difficult aspect of school was the requirement to learn to speak English. I never felt I had a good command of English, as Yupik was our native language whenever we were not at school. In our common speaking, we would use our native words. I was not completely convinced that book knowledge was very important for me to learn. I was a person more concerned about living the subsistence lifestyle than what was taught to me from books. I always considered my Pa as my teacher. He taught me the ways of living outdoors and how to subsist off the land. I spent most of my youthful life following Pa and learning from him. I tried to be a good son and obey Pa and Ma's commands.

My Pa and Ma spent all of their time in the school building during the flood, assisting my grandpa and grandma with their needs. This is the one time of the year when everyone in the village shelters in the school building. No one is left to live in their cabin, as it is too dangerous a risk of drowning from the rising flood waters.

It is a time for visiting among the adults—a time to recount the past trapping season during the winter. The men share their success or failure on their traplines: who caught the largest fox and lynx, and their number of catches. I am sure some of the stories that are shared become a little embellished, to see who could tell the biggest story. There is always the retelling of actual events that occurred while running the traplines, which required an overnight stay in the cold and snow.

My Pa recounts his experiences on the trapline. Since I spent much time with Pa on the trapline, I can share my experiences as proof of what Pa says.

My Pa's name is Unozroak. He is the son of Apak, my grandpa, and Apak's oldest son. Unozroak acts as the elder of the village, as his subsistence skills are acknowledged by everyone. He is a very skilled hunter, fisherman, and trapper. His subsistence skills provide food for everyone in the village when some families are in need. They can depend on Pa to provide when he is asked. Apak taught my Pa well and made my Pa a strong man well versed in the Yupik ways. Pa can only speak in the Yupik language, as he never went to school.

He is very accomplished at building kayaks, dogsleds, and fish traps. Again, he learned these skills from Apak. His woodworking expertise is known not only in the village but throughout the Kusquqvak region. People from upriver and downriver come to him with their wood-making needs. His patience at wood bending results in excellence and a well-made product.

Pa is a very good dog keeper and manages them as if they were a part of the family. He makes certain they are well fed, watered, and comfortable with plenty of grass to keep them warm and dry. My Pa is a good dog handler, as each dog knows its place in the team for the long journeys required in the winter.

When it comes to spiritual aspects of life, he differs with people in significant ways. While most believe in traditional medicine and shamanism, he is not convinced of the traditional stories of creation but believes a supreme being is responsible for the creation of our heaven, earth, and people. His belief in a supreme creation puts him at odds with his brothers and sister. They are very involved during potlatches to promote shamanism and medicine ceremonies.

The traditional stories they tell are, as Pa would say, "Just not believable." His brothers and sister do not argue with him to keep peace in the family and respect his elder position in the village.

My Ma's name is Arnack. She is a typical Yupik wife and mother to her family. She possesses a very friendly personality and is well liked by everyone in the village. She sacrifices her needs to provide for any of us kids or the needs of anyone in the village. She is a wonderful example to the village as the wife of the elder. She always stands by my Pa's side in cases of difference of opinion.

She performs all the cooking tasks but allows my younger sister, Nayagaq, to help so she can learn for herself. Cooking is her pride and joy in life. She makes certain every detail of food preparation is exact and perfect for her family's consumption. She allows Nayagaq to do the dish cleaning with my younger sister, Algaq, providing what help she can. Ma is very proud of the clean cabin she provides for her family. Because of this, she does most of the cabin cleaning herself. The cleaning of the cook stove she leaves for Pa. Pa has no issues with taking on the chore. We use the cookstove every day, and the accumulation of ashes has to be removed daily.

Ma is very skilled in skin sewing to make all of our clothing items. Her mother taught her well according to the native traditions. She takes great care to sew each item so they not only fit comfortably but look fancy. She most enjoys bead work, so each piece of clothing stands out when worn. Pa makes certain each skin of rabbit, fox, wolf, lynx, and moose is completely tanned and ready for Ma to prepare. She does most of her sewing during the winter, as it provides more quiet time from the summer and fall busy season. She is also very concerned about each of our personal hygiene. We kids think she is a bit over-reactive to our cleanliness. Kids get dirty—it is who we are.

Ma was born and raised in the downriver village of Kwigamuit. Her marriage with Pa was arranged between the two families. It was normal to have arranged marriages in the lower Kusquqvak region downriver from Kagemuit among the Yupik people. Arranged marriages were not common above Kwigamuit. I never knew why this type of marriage was required downriver from Kagemuit but not upriver. She would talk about how afraid she was to move to Kagemuit with Pa and leave the only family and relatives she had known since birth. My grandpa, Apak, and grandma, Emak, made her feel very loved and welcomed her as a part of the family.

Ma was well taught in the Yupik ways and was eager to help with and learn from my grandma. Her only language was Yupik. Like Pa, she did not have the opportunity to go to any school and learn another language. She is always gentle and treats all of us kids with dignity and love. We all try to show her our love in return.

She had grown up around the strong belief of medicine, shamans, and traditional stories of creation. She was quickly convinced that Pa's wisdom of a supreme being responsible for creation made a lot of sense to her.

Eventually, Pa built a cabin of his own for the two of them. They were then able to live apart from his parents and brothers and sister. He built their cabin next to grandpa's cabin. I really enjoy being so close to them.

I have a sister, Nayagaq. She is two years younger than me. She finished her time at school one year ago. She really did not like going to school but went anyway because Ma wanted her to go. She did not want to go against Ma's wishes. Nayagaq would rather stay home and learn from her Ma the way of Yupik women. She is a good, enthusiastic helper with fish cutting, berry picking, skin sewing, and assisting however she can with cooking.

While my sister is also confined to the school during the flood, she interacts with her nieces, sharing games. String shaped like a circle and held between the fingers of each hand allows one to make designs. This becomes a competition to see who can make the fanciest designs. There is also the girl talk between them to discuss what they have sewn in making various clothes for themselves and other family members. Nayagaq has a younger sister, Algaq, who requires her to care for and look after her needs while also confined in the school building during the flood.

A favorite part of being confined in the school is the opportunity to get together with my nephews and discuss our outdoor adventures with each other that occurred prior to the flood. My brother, Anngaq, who is four years younger than me, always wants to be a part of our "big boy" discussions. Anngaq has one year left in school. He is a good student, as he possesses a good mind that absorbs all the book knowledge from his schoolwork. I would say he has better than average intelligence and is not an outdoor person like me. Pa has to talk hard to get him to go outdoors with him. He does like working with the dogs, as he takes responsibility to cook fish for the dogs to eat. He makes certain each doghouse is taken good care of and has plenty of grass. School is his real treat in life, and he is a teacher's favorite. The teachers remark what a nice, well-behaved young man he is. They know his love for reading books, and his teachers keep him well stocked with ones to read. Before they left for their summer homes, each teacher gave him plenty of books to read during the summer school break. He brings his newfound books to fish camp and occupies his time reading them. Sometimes his reading has to be interrupted when he is needed to help with fishing activities that require the whole family. Pa is not convinced

Anngaq is going to make a very good subsistence provider when he marries. Pa says, "He will need to marry an old, well-established woman who will be able to take care of him."

Also confined in the school building are my youngest brother, Kuvak, and my youngest sister, Algaq, both of whom had spent much time in the building during the school year that had completed its teaching just a couple of weeks earlier. Kuvak had just finished his third year and Algaq her first year in school. They both enjoy being included in the flood watch along with their other nieces and nephews as fellow classmates. To them, the school building is now a place to run free and play hide and seek in the now empty classrooms.

The school kitchen can now be used to feed their every passion for snacks. It takes stern convincing to keep them from gorging on the endless amount of peanut butter and jelly available in the kitchen, left over from the previous school year. They eat peanut butter and jelly right out of the jar without using a pilot cracker. After finishing with their eating, they go to grandma and have her clean their messy fingers and faces. They are grandma and grandpa's favorites.

After what seemed like an eternity—but it only lasted a few days—the river water began to recede and allowed everyone to leave the school building and return to their own cabin. The arduous work of cleaning our cabin from the effects of the flood was about to begin.

Chapter 2

We were happy to finally be able to leave the school building. It was fun for a while, but it didn't take long for boredom to set in and the desire for the outdoors to grow. Each family gathered their personal belongings they had brought to the school building to take back to their cabin.

As we stepped out of the school building, the ground was very muddy with numerous puddles of water everywhere. The little kids enjoyed jumping and splashing in each one. Each family knew everyone needed to be prepared for the mud, so there were plenty of rubber boots for everyone.

The Kusquqvak River means "big river with small flow" in the Yupik language. There was still some ice with a few large icebergs floating by the village. A lot of driftwood comes from upriver during each flood season. People try to hook them from the shore and bring them to the beach. There we cut them to the correct size and split them for heat and cooking using a hand saw and axe. We need a lot of driftwood year-round to fire our cookstove.

The flood eroded the riverbank, endangering any cabin built too close to the river's edge. We knew that someday grandpa's cabin would need to be moved, as each flood season eroded the riverbank near his cabin. Each flood reshaped the river channels. This rerouting of the river caused some sloughs to go dry, and over time they were no longer navigable even with our kayaks.

As a result, some villages had to be moved. Sometimes ice jams downriver would cause the water to rise and cause even more flood damage.

With everyone now back to their cabins, the process of cleanup began. The first cabin to be cleaned belonged to grandpa and grandma. It was the right thing to do, as we all worked to provide for them first. We wanted them to be the first to occupy their cabin.

My grandpa's name is Apak, and grandma is called Emak. They first lived in a village that is now abandoned, downriver from Kagemuit. They lived among other Eskimos from other parts of the Kusquqvak region. Their village was periodically raided by people from the northern tundra. These raids resulted in Yupik men being killed and women taken hostage. Personal items such as kayaks, sleds, fish traps, and nets were stolen along with dried fish. To escape the raids, Apak and Emak loaded their kayaks and left for upriver. Their destination was unknown. They just wanted to get away from the raids that occurred too often. Apak and Emak left in one kayak and towed a second kayak loaded with their personal belongings.

After days of paddling upriver and running short of food, they decided they had gone far enough to avoid the tundra raiders. They came to a slough that grandpa thought would give them a safe and productive location to restart their lives. Apak and Emak agreed this would be a good site to settle. Apak called the site Kagemuit, which in his words meant "a place by the slough." I am not certain if that is the meaning in actual native language, but who am I to challenge my grandpa.

Once we got grandpa's cabin cleaned and ready for them to occupy, we put our effort into preparing our cabin, which was just next door. The first step during cleanup was to clean the cabin of all the accumulated mud from within. It was a terribly dirty and painstaking job with a lot of hard work removing the mud. Once the mud was removed, we could actually make the cabin livable.

The cookstove was next to be cleaned and made operable. All of us placed this as a high priority, as we all wanted to have our own cooked meal after being confined to the school building during the flood. With the cookstove ready to use, we focused our work effort on unloading the kayaks with our personal items and other belongings we had placed on the roof in boxes.

Prior to the flood, the kayaks were tied up close to the cabin and secured. We unpacked the boxes of items that belonged in the cabin from where they had been put on the roof or in our kayaks. We had four kayaks we used to hold our personal belongings and covered with tarps. Our ten dogs were put in the kayaks along with items they could not destroy. All other items that did not fit in the kayaks were placed on the cabin roof and now needed to be taken down. The dog sleds were also put on the roof so they would not float away during the flood.

The dog yard was cleaned of excess mud. Each doghouse had to be cleaned just like our cabin. Anngaq took the lead in making each doghouse ready by adding grass to each one to make them comfortable and dry. He would feed the dogs by starting a fire in the kettle and cooking fish for them. The dogs were very happy to have a fresh meal, as they were very hungry after having no food for several days while they were forced to live in the kayaks during the flood. Once the dogs had their lives brought back to normal, our work of cleaning up after the flood was complete. Now we focused our attention on my uncles' and aunt's cabins to help them with the cleanup they required.

My uncle Kevig was my Pa's next younger brother. His cabin was located beyond grandpa's cabin and next to the slough. He and his wife Ukurraq had four children. Ukurraq grew up in a now abandoned village above where we go berry picking. Eventually, over the years of flooding, the Kusquqvak River eroded its main channel, which resulted in the Atsiyar slough becoming no longer navigable above our berry picking site. The people who lived in that village had to move, and that is how Kevig met Ukurraq. Kevig went to assist the villagers in their move, and the two became close friends and eventually married. Ukurraq is also Yupik and is very adept in the Eskimo ways, as her family were good subsistence people. I was always interested in hearing her stories about her growing up as a little girl on the tundra. It was a life very different from ours living on a big river. Her village was very isolated, as it was located at the end of a very long and winding slough. I never tired of listening to her stories from such a different land from mine.

I especially enjoyed her story regarding their attempts to herd reindeer. While she was very young, white traders thought it would be a good idea to start a reindeer herd near her village. According to the white people, only natives could herd the reindeer. Her Pa was one of the men in the village who volunteered his help. The village was promised the venture would be very successful and help the village prosper. The program did not work as intended because the Yupik people are fishermen, hunters, and trappers. They are not agricultural animal herders, and when fishing and berry picking season began, the reindeer were not a priority. Over time, her village began to lose the reindeer from neglect, and the operation failed.

Their oldest son, Kenruk, was my best friend in the village. He was my age, and we finished school the same year. We tended to have much in common. He was a person who desired to be outdoors with his Pa, just as I did. We enjoyed making toy boats and racing them in the slough to see who had made the fastest one.

During the winter we built igloos near the cabin. This would prove important when caught out in the tundra overnight. Kenruk and I were always the best when we played hopscotch with the other kids. We played lap games with all the kids in the village. Kenruk and I would choose teams since we were the best players and always the team captains. The game is played with a bat and ball and two teams. The bat was no more than a driftwood stick and a ball someone brought from their cabin. One team played as fielders and one team as batters. Two lines are made with a stick about thirty yards apart. Each team stands behind the lines. A pitcher lobs a ball to the batter. Once the ball is hit, the runner runs as fast as possible to the opposite line without being hit by the ball that was retrieved by a player from the opposite team. The runner has to run back to the batter line to score.

We competed against each other to see who could make the best slingshot. We pretended to be on a bird hunt and see who could hit a bird we made out of mud from the slough. When we were not at our own cabin, the two of us would be found together.

They also had two daughters, Teruluk and Nayak, and a son named Cetaaq. I really never spent much time with the two girls. They played girl games between themselves. Cetaaq was much younger and actually spent more time with his sisters than with Kenruk and me.

Since Kevig and Ukurraq were just a short walk from our cabin, we could visit them often. My Pa got along very well with Kevig. Kevig would consult with Pa regarding the construction of his kayak and dogsled repairs. Pa built the kayaks and dogsleds Kevig used. Kevig would promise Pa he would someday take the time to have Pa show him how to bend wood and cut and shape the pieces, but the time never seemed to come.

Grandpa spent much time with Pa during his younger years teaching him all his outdoor skills. This made Pa the elder Kevig would consult for the skills needed for subsistence life.

I liked my uncle Kevig, as he treated me with respect and appreciation of my own outdoor skills. I was able to share my hunting adventures with him. He appreciated the fact that I spent time with his son Kenruk. He encouraged me to teach him all the skills I have learned. I like the way he also looked at me as more mature than I thought I was.

My Pa and Kevig usually treated each other with much respect and were amenable. They did differ regarding each other's thoughts and stands concerning shamanism, medicine, and creation stories. Kevig was a strong believer in these positions while Pa had strong beliefs in a supreme being. They would not argue with angry voices but would simply agree to disagree. If any discussion turned to that topic, both Kevig and Pa would respectfully decline to enter the talk.

The beliefs Kevig held were also the same as my other uncle, Arlunaq, and aunt Qavcik. Both of them had very strong beliefs as did Kevig, but while Kevig would not argue his points, they were quick to espouse their beliefs and would argue strongly about their position. After too many arguments between Pa and Arlunaq and Qavcik ended in a shouting match, Pa became detached from their family.

My family went to Kevig's cabin to check in with them to see if they needed any help with post-flood cleanup. They were mostly finished with the cleanup except for getting the dogs organized. I was happy to assist with that chore along with my brother Anngaq, who cooked the first meal for the dogs. Anngaq also made certain each doghouse was clean and had fresh grass taken from the smokehouse. Anngaq was happy to help his uncle and was treated to a pilot cracker with butter for his efforts. It made our entire family feel good to assist other families as they recovered from the effects of the flood.

My aunt Qavcik lived on the other side of the slough. Cakiraq, Qavcik's husband, had built a foot bridge across the slough to access their cabin.

Before the foot bridge was built, we had to get in our kayak to access the other side. During late fall, when the water level in the slough fell enough, we could run and jump across without getting wet. Obviously, without the bridge, the older ones were not able to simply walk to visit them. Cakiraq came over to our cabin to inform Pa that his dogsled had come loose from its tie-down on the roof and broke when it fell to the ground. Pa needed to check out the extent of the damage and determine how to repair it. Pa was able to make a few new wood bends and replace the broken ones on Cakiraq's sled. He was very happy Pa was able to repair it for use again.

Cakiraq met aunt Qavcik when she went to a potlatch in the village of Kameglimiut. Kameglimiut is an upriver village beyond where we go to fish camp. Cakiraq is also Yupik. His family was one of the older ones in the village. His Pa believed strongly in the Eskimo stories of creation and was a powerful shaman respected by the village people. He was not a strong outdoorsman and relied on others in the village to help with his family support. As a result, he did not teach Cakiraq the skills needed to be a successful native provider.

Actually, my aunt Qavcik taught him the ways of subsistence she learned by watching my grandpa, Apak. Apak felt sorry for Cakiraq and provided him with the necessary kayaks, dogsleds, and fish traps his family would require.

Qavcik and Cakiraq had two sons, Tanek and Tanguq, and a daughter, Qilak. They were the same age as my younger brother and sister, so I did not interact with them much. I would occasionally be told by Ma to take my younger brother and sister over to play with Qavcik's children. I did it to obey Ma, but really didn't want to do it. While they played, I would cross over the bridge and see if Kenruk was home, and we would do activities outside so I could keep an eye on the younger ones. Kenruk knew my reasoning and went along with my makeshift babysitting. Qavcik's children came out to participate when we all played together as village kids.

My other uncle, Arlunaq, lived next to the slough on our side. His wife's name is Kiak. They did not have any children. I did not visit them much since they had no kids. Arlunaq had a natural intelligence that always amazed me. He was a deep thinker. He saw the world in a different way from the rest of us. His cabin was a good example of his unusual creativity. Rather than placing the logs on top of each other, he stood them upright. It looked odd and very out of place but seemed to work. He was the best English-speaking one among his brothers and sister. He used words I had no idea what they meant. Many times, Pa would return from visiting him and say, "I just don't know where he gets all his ideas. They just don't make sense to me according to our native way." His wife Kiak seemed to understand him completely, though.

She came from upriver one day in a canoe during the summer. We knew she came from far away and from a different group of people, as what she paddled looked like a kayak but was not built like one. She stopped at our village as a rest stop. We invited her into our cabin and gave her some coffee and akutaq. She had never eaten akutaq, and we knew for sure she had come from far away. Her speech was foreign with a mix of an unusual blend of Yupik. She told us she was a mix of Yupik and Upriver Indian. She was able to also speak English very well. By her speaking and using words we don't use, we knew she was well educated.

Arlunaq took a liking to her instantly the moment they met. She was very good looking, so I could see why he admired her. The fact that she had a good education was one reason Arlunaq took to her. They had a lot in common, as she, according to us, was a deep thinker just like Arlunaq. We knew they were destined for each other, and they were soon married. They built their unusual cabin along the slough and away from the rest of us. They desired their privacy and it was a show of their expression that they were "different" from the rest of the village residents.

I most enjoyed listening to Kiak talk about her life in her village. I eventually had the courage to inquire why she left her village and came downriver by herself. She explained that her mother often talked about how she missed her Yupik family. Kiak then decided to take it upon herself to go downriver and try to find her native Eskimo roots. I thought it was very brave of a young woman to embark upon such a journey. I am happy she did, as I like her very much. She added a new personality to our village.

Her village is located at the junction of the Kusquqvak River, between the Yupik and Upriver Indian people. That is why Kiak is half Yupik from her Ma and half Indian from her Pa. She would talk about going moose hunting with her Pa very near her village. They had built a moose camp with a cabin and a cache to prevent bears from getting after the meat. It sounded like a real outdoorsman paradise located among tall trees and marshy lakes. Shortly after her marriage with Arlunaq, he, Pa, and Kiak would go upriver to her village and hunt moose every fall. Having moose meat really added to our diet, and having moose hide to tan and use for sewing was very welcomed by Ma. Moose hide made excellent parkas. Adding a wolf ruff to the collar created a parka that was very warm and functional. I will admit Kiak has become a wonderful addition to our village and family unit. Her presence opened up a whole new world for us to explore.

Now that all the family cabins have been cleaned and made ready to occupy, we can get our lives back to normal. Looking forward to the return of salmon in the river means our next stage in our cycle of life is to prepare for this year's fishing season and life at fish camp.

Chapter 3

Now that the village is cleaned of the effects of the flood and everyone's cabin is ready for everyday living, we start to prepare for travel to fish camp.

While we waited for the river to lower from its flood level and watched its flow come to a calmer condition, we played games and went to grandpa's cabin as often as Pa would allow. Sometimes we would sneak over to grandpa's cabin without Pa's permission. When Pa would show his disapproval, grandpa would take our side and say, "Oh, they are just kids and enjoy visiting us."

With my brothers and sisters, we use sticks and draw a hopscotch game in the always wet riverbank dirt. I really like the running and jumping that the game requires. A good sense of balance is also needed. It helps us develop the skills needed for our way of life outdoors. I am respectful of my youngest brother and sister being younger than I and not as skillful at playing the game. I do not always play my best, so that they can win sometimes. They gloat that they beat their older brother. On other occasions I try my best and win. They do not handle losing very well and run to Ma for comfort. The area in front of our cabin makes for easy etching of a hopscotch layout. If it doesn't rain, the layout can last for days. Then we play it often until it eventually fades and a new one needs to be made. Kuvak and Algaq especially enjoy jump rope. Nayagaq and Anngaq swing the rope and let Kuvak and Algaq take turns jumping. My role as the oldest big brother is to count each one's jumps to see who the winner would be. Sometimes I purposely miscount, and whoever is jumping yells to me, "Qataruaq, count right!"

When we are not playing games, we sneak off to grandpa's cabin. If we go early in the morning, we can talk grandpa into making pancakes for us. He makes great ones that are just the right consistency and flavor. Grandpa makes syrup out of a mixture of sugar and water. Grandma happily sits on the side of her bed and watches us enjoy our breakfast. Grandma is a great cook, but pancakes are always made by grandpa.

While eating our pancakes, grandpa entertains us with his stories about his outdoor experiences while hunting, fishing, and trapping. Subsistence life is difficult, and under the best conditions, situations can turn bad. Life on the river requires a sense of watching the weather, as you do not want to get caught in a sudden storm. The big waves can easily turn a kayak over in the water. When grandpa's stories start to get a little overwhelming, grandma speaks up and says, "You know you are making it bigger than it really was." Grandpa acknowledges and says, "But it sure felt like it at the time." Grandma is one who desires the truth and only the truth. She has a very strong sense of ethics. All Eskimo grandmas seem to be that way.

Once the river flow begins to calm and return to normal, it is time for us to use kayaks. Before we can spend the summer at fish camp, we need to purchase the necessary provisions.

That requires a half-day trip by kayak to the village of Mamimuit. This is the location of the nearest store. By this time of year, the daylight makes for lots of sunshine for travel on the river. We take two kayaks with us. Ma and Pa ride in one and I follow in the second. My kayak is loaded with furs that we caught in our traps during the winter trapping season. We will trade the furs for food that we need. It has been a very good year on the trapline, and we are planning to purchase more than usual. It has been a good year for both quantity and quality of furs. The furs should provide us top dollar to trade for food and other necessary items that we need. Even after keeping enough furs for tanning that Ma can use for sewing, we still have an ample supply to trade at the store.

We leave my other brothers and sisters at grandma's cabin. Although having four extra people in her cabin, grandma is always happy and excited to have them during the time we will be gone. She loves all her grandchildren very much. She knows that we will purchase food to share with them also. That always helps pay for the extra burden that she has to endure.

We observe the morning weather and decide it is good to depart. Ma and Pa shove off in their kayak and I follow in my kayak loaded with furs. It is a half-day's journey downriver that allows us to go quickly and easily. About halfway to Mamimuit is the village of Kwigamuit. We always have to stop here and visit Ma's parents and grandparents. This is where Ma was born and raised, and she enjoys the opportunity to visit whenever she can.

As we land our kayaks on the beach, we are met by one of Arnack's nieces. She is so excited to see Arnack and invites us to her cabin. At her parents' cabin we are invited to have tea. It is a customary gesture to have tea and dried fish over a good time of family talk.

Pa and I talk with her brother and share our trapping experience during the past winter. It was a good trapping season for the Kwigamuit people also. It was an especially good year for trapping wolves. Pa and I are envious to hear the success the people experienced with trapping so many wolves. With an unusually cold winter, the fur on the wolves was extra dense, so the quality was better than usual. Arnack's brother knows that we are going to trade furs at the Mamimuit store and gives us one of his wolf pelts to add to our supply. He says he has more than enough and wants to share his success with his sister. He figures Arnack will probably keep it for herself and add it to her sewing supply of furs once Pa tans it for use. He is correct—Ma keeps it and does not allow us to trade it. This will be her prize, and no one is going to take it from her. She is very excited to receive it and sew it into a garment that someone can wear.

After enjoying our visit with her brother's family, we walk over to her parents' cabin. Her parents are about the same age as my grandparents. They are very excited to see us and especially their daughter. We have to accept their invitation of coffee and pilot crackers with shortening—a Yupik staple for traditional diet. Both her parents are experiencing some health issues, as the winter cold has not been kind to them. They are resigned to the fact that they are not able to get out much and enjoy the outdoors. This is disappointing for Ma to hear, and she worries that their condition could get worse. She is confident that her brothers and sisters in the village will take good care of them if needed. If their condition gets worse, they can be taken to Mamimuit, which has a doctor's office there.

I always enjoy our visits with her parents. There is never enough time to visit, but we have to depart in order to arrive in Mamimuit before darkness makes traveling on the river difficult and dangerous. It is very hard to see the sandbars at night. We say our goodbyes and Arnack hugs both her parents and departs with a kiss from each other. We leave in our kayaks with an unexpected addition of a very fine wolf pelt from my uncle.

As we depart in our kayaks, we are sent off with almost all of Ma's brothers and sisters standing on the riverbank waving their farewells. The children, as usual, stand on the riverbank and continue to wave until we are out of their sight. The portion of our journey from Kwigamuit to Mamimuit is about one quarter of our total journey. The river begins to widen as we continue downriver, which makes for fewer waves but with a slower current. It is safer but requires more paddling to maintain our speed.

It seems the further we go, the longer it takes. My patience always tends to wear thin until the village comes into view. It always seems as though we are about to run out of daylight just when we see the village ahead. We land our kayaks in front of the village, which happens to be right next to the store. The village of Mamimuit is much larger than any of the villages in our section of the river. Mamimuit is a central connection to both upriver and downriver villages. It has stores, a doctor's office, and a church as part of the village community. Overall, Mamimuit is a very large village with a very diverse group of people that live there. It also has a river port where large steamboats from as far away as Seattle are able to dock and deliver goods that are required by a much larger village.

After we pull our kayaks onto the shore and tie them up, we walk to the store to welcome ourselves inside. This is not just any store, as it also is home to my uncle Tagneq. Tagneq is my Pa's youngest brother. Maybe it is because he was the youngest that he never really seemed to fit in with the rest of his brothers and sister. While the others were learning about the subsistence life, he wanted to be his own person. I don't think it was rebellion—just that grandpa and grandma were okay with him choosing a different path in his life. He did have the gift of woodworking like Pa. He could make very strong and durable dogsleds, kayaks, and fish traps. Rather than use them for his own use, he would sell them to people that would travel by our village. He had a real gift of gab to convince people to buy his creations.

Whenever we traveled to Mamimuit to buy goods at the Northern Commercial Company store, he would use the opportunity to barter with the residents to trade his woodwork for whatever he could get in return. It worked out well for grandpa and grandma, as he would come back to the village with household goods of all kinds for Emak. She really enjoyed his trades that brought home more furs for her to sew. Tagneq soon became her favorite and looked forward to his return from every trip to see what he had brought with him. Apak was also very happy when he returned with items that he could use. He would trade for guns, ammunition, and animal traps, and to see the joy in grandpa's eyes was priceless.

Tagneq was kept busy building his woodworking supply while the other brothers were providing for their subsistence needs. We all knew that someday he would desire to leave Kagemuit and make his own life in Mamimuit. It was hard to see him leave, but we knew it was best for him. He would be a success having more people to trade with downriver where the population was greater.

Tagneq met a Yupik lady named Nuliaq and eventually they were married. Nuliaq was the daughter of one of the Northern Commercial Company managers. Rather than working for the company, Tagneq started his own store in another part of the village away from Northern Commercial. Nuliaq was helpful during the startup of their store with what she had observed from watching her Pa working at his store. They called the store "Yupik Trading Post," and people from their side of the village and those downriver came to the store to trade. He continued his woodworking as a business that proved to be very successful. The quality of his work became very well known throughout the Kusquqvak River delta. People from across the region came to trade for his creations. His store sold mostly groceries and items that were used in cooking and housekeeping. That worked out great for us, as it was the staple food that we most needed. He also bought and traded furs. This put him in direct competition with Northern Commercial, which also traded and bought furs. Tagneq had worked a deal with the best Seattle fur buyers, which allowed him to pay more for the furs that he took as a trade.

After we bring our kayaks onto the beach and secure them, we carry our furs for trading up to the store. Tagneq and Nuliaq meet us at the front door of the store and greet us with warm hugs. Tagneq takes the furs and remarks how good quality they are. "I can offer you top dollar trades for the entire batch," says Tagneq. "I can offer you a premium price for that wolf pelt," he says. Arnack is quick to reply, "Oh no, the wolf pelt goes back with me to Kagemuit. It is not for trade, as I will make that into a very warm parka," states Ma with a very possessive tone in her voice. She remarks that it was a gift from her brother when we stopped to visit at Kwigamuit. "That should make a very fine parka with your gifted sewing hands," says Nuliaq. She hints a little envy that she would like one. We stack the furs in a pile near the fur buying counter. There are already several large piles of furs behind the counter from the day's trading activity. Tagneq is certainly doing very well in the fur trading business.

We walk up the stairs that lead to their living quarters. I always think it is very convenient that the building is two stories tall with the store on the main level and their cabin upstairs. The store is not made of logs but is sided on the outside with a horizontal lap siding look. He must have purchased the siding from a Seattle or Anchorage lumber company. The inside is covered with very fancy boards that actually fit together and overlap each other. The same boards are used on the ceiling as well. There is no walking into the weather to get to the store. Once we get to the top of the stairs, I am quickly met by Tungay, one of their sons. Tungay and I are very good friends. We are best buddies. We are the same age, and he is a very good outdoorsman and knows the Yupik ways as good as anyone. He is a very proficient fisherman and trapper, as he helps us at fish camp in the summer and runs the trapline with us in the winter. He will return with us to Kagemuit with his kayak and go to help us at fish camp. He is a great addition with his skills at fishing.

As soon as we are all upstairs, we visit over coffee, tea, and akutaq. Akutaq is called Eskimo ice cream. It is made from blueberries, salmon, Crisco shortening, seal oil, and sugar. We do not always have access to seal oil, as we live too far upriver to harvest seal. A box of pilot crackers is always open and available for the taking. Tungay and I grab our share and go off to his room to have our own time together. It is a real opportunity for a son, like Tungay, to have his own room just for him. It even has a door that we close to give us even more privacy. There are photographs on his wall that were taken with a camera of him in various outdoor settings. Obviously, we cannot afford a camera, so looking at his photographs is a unique experience.

Tungay has a younger brother named Nakiak and a younger sister named Tengmiaq. Each has a room to themselves. I think they sure have the luxury of having their own room. How different from the one-room cabin that my entire family lives in at Kagemuit. It is very apparent that Tagneq and Nuliaq are very rich by our native standards. Their lifestyle is so different from ours. Tagneq has done very well after leaving our village when he did. After Tungay and I eat our fill of akutaq spread on pilot crackers, we run downstairs with his younger brother and sister following close behind. They do not want to be left out of whatever we are going to do. Even though it is almost midnight, the sun has not set, and we play several hopscotch games before we all tire out. It is bedtime and we need plenty of rest for our trip back to Kagemuit.

The next morning Nuliaq prepares a breakfast of pancakes, eggs, and bacon. It is all new to us, as she makes the pancakes from a mix in a box. She does not have to mix flour and water to make them like grandpa. Her eggs are store-bought ones from chickens, where our eggs are what we find on the tundra from ducks and geese. The only time we ever have bacon is when we come to her home. She knows we miss having bacon and that it is a real treat for us. There is a very noticeable difference between our meal preparation and what aunt Nuliaq provides us when we visit. Tagneq and Nuliaq certainly live a very different life from what we live in Kagemuit.

After breakfast it is time to trade our furs for the provisions that we need for fish camp. Our food needs are just the basics, including condensed milk, flour, sugar, pilot crackers, shortening, coffee, tea, and rice. We need Clorox to purify the water at fish camp. We will complement those items with the fish that we catch, eggs we gather from the tundra, and any birds that we catch when we have the time to take our guns with us.

We settle our trade agreements for our items, then carry them to our kayaks for loading. Tungay comes with us back to Kagemuit. We say our goodbyes, and Tungay hugs his parents and brother and sister. He will spend the summer with us and away from his family. As we push our kayaks into the water, we notice that a steamship has arrived from Seattle during the night. It brought not only goods destined for both stores in the village but also passengers. People from far away lands come to Mamimuit to live and do business. The people of Mamimuit are a very diverse group that includes many different nationalities. People with skin colors that I have never seen anywhere else except here in Mamimuit. Because of its connections with the outside world, it is the center of activity for this section of the river.

The three of our kayaks shove off from the shore and head upriver back to home. Going upriver is certainly more challenging and much harder, as we have to paddle against the current. It was a half-day journey downriver, but most of the day to make the trip back to our home.

Chapter 4

After our return from the Mamimuit resupply trip, we waited a couple of weeks, then began our journey to fish camp.

During this time, Tungay and I assisted Pa in preparing the fish nets. Some needed a few repairs to mend any cut or broken mesh. We used twine to repair and mend the tears that fish made in the nets during last fishing season. The large tears had to be mended so that smaller fish could not just swim through. I watched Pa perform his magic of transforming a worn and torn net into one that was as good as new. A fish net was a critical piece of fishing gear that was required for us to carry on our native way of life. We valued them greatly.

Whenever possible, we would take advantage of the returning waterfowl. We would take our guns and kayaks up the Kagemuit slough that leads to the open tundra. We would stop our kayaks when we spotted a lake that would be a good magnet for the waterfowl that would be drawn to it. Many different species of ducks, teals, geese, swans, and loons were found around the tundra lakes. My family was very excited when we would return with some birds.

During the evenings with nothing to do, we went to the communal house, or in Yupik we called the qasgiq. It was a gathering place for the village. Some evenings it was designated for sauna use. The men and boys would use it first, then the women and girls would follow when the men finished. Taking a sauna was a competition for some. The central fire pit housed a container which contained water. The steam is what created the sauna effect that made our bodies begin sweating. The sweating was good, as it removed the poisons from our skin. The competition would begin when someone started pouring water and making the steam heat grow. How long could you tolerate the heat before you had to leave? I could not tolerate much heat, so I was the first to leave. Pa was always able to outlast me in the sauna.

Some evenings it was used for sessions called "wise words," where grandpa would come and teach the young people our native ways of living. This period of teaching was called qanruyutet. My grandpa acted as the most elder of our village since he was the oldest. My Pa also acted as the village elder when grandpa felt he could not fulfill that position. My Pa was the oldest brother, so he was next in line to succeed him as elder of the village. These "wise word" sessions are very important to instill in the younger ones the importance of respect for each other and teach the right and wrong of life.

When the qasgiq was designated for Eskimo stories of creation and shamanism, my grandpa and Pa refused to attend. They did not believe in the supernatural nature of the Eskimo stories that were told.

Prior to departure to fish camp, Tungay and I visited my uncles' cabins to see if they needed our help to prepare for fishing season. They were grateful for our help and would tell us what we could do to assist. Every family left for their own fish camp. The entire village would be vacated except for grandpa and grandma. Everyone located their fish camp near the big eddy, which is where we also fished. Usually, we would head to fish camp about two weeks after the flood waters receded. It was getting time to go, and our anxiety grew with each passing day.

To prepare for departure for fish camp, we would pull our kayaks close to the cabin. We had five kayaks with Ma and Pa in one, me, Anngaq, Tungay, and one extra that would be towed. We loaded our camp food, cooking utensils, pots and pans, and a Yukon stove for heat and cooking. A canvas tent, blankets, fish nets, buoys, and anchors. We made certain we brought along our guns and ammunition. The dogs and kettle for cooking fish were loaded in the kayak that was towed.

Fish camp was one full day's journey upriver. Going against the current required a lot of hard paddling since our kayaks were very full of fish camp gear. We stopped at midday to have lunch along the riverbank of dried fish and tea. We arrived during early evening at our fish camp site, which is a short distance downriver from the big eddy where we set our nets.

We pulled up to the riverbank and needed to cut steps into the cut bank to get up to the top. If the flood was not too violent, there would still be steps and leftover clothes poles, fish racks, our smokehouse, drying racks, and cutting table. If they were washed away during the flood, then we had to make new ones from the available driftwood. We put up the white canvas wall tent first. It served as the center of our universe at camp. The Yukon stove went up next. The food items, cooking utensils, and bedding were placed in one corner of the tent.

The dogs are staked away from the camp area. Once the dogs are cared for by Anngaq, we are ready to settle in and care for ourselves with our first meal at fish camp.

After our meal, Tungay and I went exploring around camp. We were curious to see what may have changed from last year. In the past there was a large lake nearby that usually drew a large bird concentration for potential hunting opportunities. When we approached the lake, we saw many birds take flight. We thought it would be a good hunting season. The lake also provided our water supply. After our exploration, we agreed it would be a good summer at fish camp. Hopefully it would be a productive fishing season also.

The next morning was our first time to go fishing. With the net, buoy, and anchor in the kayak, we set out for the opposite shore, which was a sandbar beach. We staked out the beach side of the net and maneuvered the kayak across the river toward the cut bank where we ended the net with a buoy and anchor.

We go back to fish camp and wait till evening to check for fish. We use this time to rest from the hard work of setting the net. We fire up the Yukon stove and make hot water for a cup of tea to warm up with a pilot cracker. The mornings are still cool, and a warmup from setting the net is appreciated. Ma and the girls are busy organizing the tent. They make sure that everything has a place so that we can find the items we need. The boxes that held our items during our trip to fish camp become our tent cupboards. Until the fish start hitting the nets, our day can be a little boring. When evening comes, we go back to the net and check for fish. The first few days we catch no fish.

During this time, the other Kagemuit families come to set up their fish camps. With no fish to process, we can visit the other families and help with their camp setup. These families set up camps on our side of the river because of its easy access to the large lake behind the camps.

With other families camping near us, the girls can play story knife. It seems that every time girls come together, they play story knife. It is not a game that boys participate in. My sisters always have something in their pockets to use to make etchings in the dirt that are required to play the game. They use their story knife to draw illustrations in the dirt. One girl draws a picture in the dirt while the rest of the girls look on and try to interpret the story behind the picture. Each girl gives their thoughts about what the picture means. The girl that is able to interpret the picture is then given the opportunity to draw the next picture in the dirt. Every girl has the chance to draw in the dirt with her own story knife. If a picture cannot be interpreted, then the girl responsible for the picture provides the story. It allows the girls to use their creativity and imagination. It is a game that results in the girls in the village building a lasting bond with each other.

Even older women play story knife back in the village. They meet in front of the communal house and play just like the girls. Their example provides a very good reason for the girls to meet together. Story knife creates an environment among the females of the village—a reason to meet and have a fun time among each other.

One afternoon, Algaq and Kuvak are busy making toy boats from small driftwood that they find on the riverbank. They attach string to the pieces of wood so they can drag them along the riverbank in the water. Algaq gets a little too close to the water and loses her balance and gets very wet. All her clothes are soaked with river water. She runs up the riverbank to Ma with tears in her eyes. She not only got her good clothes wet but lost the boat that she spent so much time making. Kuvak tries to grab the boat, but it floats out into the current and is lost.

After a few days of fishing, we catch our first salmon. It isn't a big catch, just a few king salmon. The king salmon is called kiagtaq in our Yupik language. It is the largest salmon and can grow to be very large and hard to handle because of its weight. It is the first to arrive and migrate the farthest upriver to spawn. It is very rich in oil and great tasting.

After checking the net and picking the salmon into our kayak, we then bring them to the beach where the fish cutting table is located. Tungay and I carry the fish from the kayak to the cutting table. My Ma and Nayagaq cut the fish. Anngaq carries the cut fish using the steps on the cut bank to Pa, who then hangs them on the drying racks. The king salmon stay on the drying racks until they look dry. Then they are carried into the smokehouse where they are hung on racks near the ceiling. This is the final curing step. A fire is made of birch wood that we carefully kept just for this purpose from the driftwood that we collected. We make certain it burns slowly so it provides the smoke that flavors the fish. I love eating smoked kiagtaq at fish camp while it is still fresh from the smokehouse.

The parts of the fish that are not kept for our consumption are separated and kept to feed the dogs. As a result, no part of the fish is wasted. Every fish is important to either our family or the dogs. The dogs eat well while they are at fish camp.

The small number of fish caught is a good start for the season, as it allows us to work out a good work routine. It is necessary to work as a team once the number of fish increases. The quantity of fish will increase dramatically as the season progresses. This routine will continue every day while the fish are "running." It is exhausting but required. We need all the kings that we can harvest to feed us throughout the winter until the next fishing season. With our upcoming hosting of the annual potlatch, we need to catch more fish than usual to feed the extra people that will come to our village. Everyone in the village is aware that many more fish are needed to be caught just to host the potlatch. Every fisherman in the village feels the added stress to catch more fish this season.

On the days when the catch is reduced, we can complete our fish cutting work early. This allows us to do other activities during the day before we check the nets again in the evening. Tungay and I take our guns and walk to the lake and try to shoot a few waterfowl. The lake is a good place to hide in the tall grass and wait for them to fly and land near us. I pride myself on being a good shot, but Tungay is a real expert with a gun. We always come back to camp with a good load of ducks that will last for several days. Once we drop the ducks off in front of the tent, Ma and my sisters go to work taking the feathers off to prepare them for cooking. They are happy to have something other than fish for the evening meal.

My youngest brother, Kuvak, and youngest sister, Algaq, spend their days playing around the camp. They are always wandering off to the tundra to pick flowers for Ma and Nayagaq. Forget-me-not flowers become the favorite flower to pick from the tundra. It is a beautiful flower with blue petals and a yellow center. These flowers give the tundra its rich and varied color. It is my Ma's favorite flower. She always loves to receive a bouquet of them.

Kuvak and Algaq are too young to help with the fish cutting duties. I do not want to be near them with an ulu cutting knife in their hands. An ulu is the half-moon shaped knife that we use for cutting fish. It makes cutting fish very quick and accurate. A very versatile Eskimo creation that my Pa made for Arnack and Nayagaq to use whenever food needs to be cut.

When Kuvak and Algaq act bored and need something to do, Ma sends them to look for eggs, wild potatoes, and greens that grow in the pond water on the tundra behind camp. This task makes them feel useful, especially when Ma praises them for a job well done. They are extra happy when asked to gather Labrador tea. Every member of our family likes that tea.

As the king salmon season ends, the next fish to arrive is the chum salmon. We call chum salmon aluyak in our Yupik language. They are smaller than king salmon and less oily, so they dry faster. The numbers of chums caught in our nets almost triple the number of kings.

Aluyak are primarily cut up as dog food, thus their other name as dog salmon. Catching dog salmon is just as important, as the dogs have to eat also. Because the number of chums is so great, the work really grows, and it seems we work all day and night to process them. The chums are only air dried on the drying racks. We do not smoke them. The sled dogs do not need their salmon smoked.

We are always tired and do not have much free time as during king season. The mosquitoes always accompany the arrival of chums. The number of mosquitoes is so great they can make life miserable. They are a terrible pest. Sometimes, it is very difficult to work because of their buzzing and biting. You cannot get away from them when outside. On a day without any wind, you can see them swarm in such great numbers that you would think it is a low-hanging cloud. Inside the tent we use smoking PIC coils to keep them outside. These smoking coils do not smell very good, but it is better than being bitten by dozens of them trying to bite at once.

It is a rare day when the chum catch is low and allows us to spend our time on other activities. During the chum run, I take my kayak and make a trip back to Kagemuit to bring Apak and Emak to fish camp. It makes them very happy to come to fish camp and be a part of the experience.

This fish camp that we occupy is the same one that Apak used when he moved to Kagemuit. When they are in camp, they are proud to share their past fish camp experiences with us. When grandpa and grandma first settled in Kagemuit, they rarely journeyed upriver. People from the upriver area would stop at Kagemuit and tell grandpa that a big eddy existed about one day's journey away. No one was fishing there, and no evidence of any fish camp activity was observed. They encouraged him to go and explore the potential as a good fishing site. Grandpa took his kayak upriver to check it out and determine if it really was a good fishing site as they stated. It did seem to have the right current flow that would make for good fishing. The surrounding area provided everything that was needed to support a fish camp. There was a large lake for fresh water and likely a good environment for waterfowl hunting. It proved to be a good location, and grandpa continued to use it until he could no longer make the trip and handle the hard work required at fish camp. He handed it to Pa to use as his own site since he was the oldest son.

His other brothers saw the big eddy area as good for fishing and set their camps nearby. With his brothers and sister nearby, it became a family fishing area for Kagemuit. It was good for support and safety to have fish camps nearby. The closeness of family made the atmosphere very family friendly for the children as well as adults.

Every summer as the chum season begins to slow, Tungay and I go upriver to the Ben Miller camp to hunt rabbits. We get to his camp by going upriver above the big eddy and before the village of Kameglimiut. It is an opportunity for Kuvak and Algaq to get out of fish camp. They become bored with staying around camp and need a change of scenery. We take two kayaks with Tungay and Kuvak in one and Algaq with me. Our real reason to get away from fish camp is to hunt rabbits. A stop at Ben Miller's camp is an excuse to see him, and he enjoys a visit from us.

Kuvak and Algaq bring along their slingshots that Pa made for them. They feel like they are contributing to the hunt with the slingshots they bring. Tungay and I bring our guns with enough ammunition in case we have a few misses from our guns. It doesn't take long paddling upriver when we spot Ben's fish net at the mouth of the slough where he lives. We enter the slough and continue our journey east toward the rising sun.

Ben's cabin is the only one on the slough, so when we see it in the distance, we know it is his. As we come closer, we see his small dog yard of four dogs before we land our kayaks in front of his cabin. His kayak is anchored in front of his cabin, so we know he is home. He overhears the young kids talking loudly and making plenty of noise because of the dogs barking at our approach.

Ben meets us at the door with his gun aimed at us as we approach. "Ben! It is Qataruaq and Tungay coming to visit you!" We both shout at the same time. Ben recognizes us and quickly lowers his gun. "You never know what is making the dogs restless. It could be a bear or wolf," he says. "Come on in and have some coffee or tea for the little ones."

The inside of his cabin is a typical old-timer setup with only the bare necessities inside. Almost all his life's possessions are stored in the cabin. Over a cup of coffee, we exchange our fishing season's progress. He states that his net has caught enough fish to feed himself and his dogs for the winter. He looks forward to the upcoming pink season that he hopes will add to his fish supply.

After we finish with our coffee and tea, he takes us out and shows us his garden that he is very proud of. His cabbage patch has very large ones and his rhubarb is gigantic. The tundra soil can grow large vegetables if worked properly. He has added soil over time from the riverbank to help make his garden more fertile. We tell him that we are on our annual rabbit hunt, and we should be on our way to get to our favorite rabbit patch. He remarks, "There are a lot of rabbits this year and they are a real problem eating my carrots." Ben says, "Shoot as many as you can to thin the population."

We get in our kayaks and continue our journey up the slough. The slough begins to narrow as we go farther. This is our indication that we are nearing the rabbit hunting grounds. The willow stands thicken and we decide that we have gone far enough. As soon as we get out of our kayak, we see several rabbits sitting among the willows. We quickly have two rabbits caught.

Kuvak and Algaq take their slingshots and walk onto the tundra in search of birds. They spend most of their time picking flowers and tundra greens. This area is very plentiful with bird eggs everywhere. Obviously, it is not frequented by humans, as the bird life is not afraid of anyone.

It does not take long to catch a lot of rabbits. We call for the little ones that we are ready to go back home. They come with their clothes full of eggs and hands holding a bunch of flowers for Ma and Nayagaq. Our trip back to fish camp is easy as we go with the current flow.

Pa is very impressed with our catch of rabbits. Ma and Nayagaq are happy to get the flowers that were picked for them. Ma will cook up the eggs during our evening meal. Ma takes me aside and tells me how quiet the camp was without the little ones around.

The chum salmon run eventually slows and is replaced with the beginning of the pink salmon migration. We call the pink salmon cuqpeq. They are the smallest of the salmon and migrate every other year. By coincidence, it is the year for the pinks. They are also called humpback because of the arched back they grow as they mature after migrating farther upriver. They can run in very large numbers. It is similar to chum season, as we seem to work all the time just to keep up with the work. Since the pinks are much smaller fish, we can process a greater number each day, so it goes quicker without as much work required per fish. Cuqpeq are only cut for dog food. We eat some pink salmon during the fall just to preserve as many king salmon as possible for winter eating.

Pink season usually means the rainy season is about to begin. It can rain and rain often during this time of year. Aside from the fact that a person seems to be wet all the time, fishing is at its best when there is rain during the setting of fish nets. The rain along with the clouds darkens the water and actually helps with the fish catch. Even the nets are not as easily seen by the fish, making them easier to catch. So, we get wet, but we catch more fish.

When the pink run is complete, that signals the end of fishing season and time to begin breaking down fish camp. It is a time to feel some sadness, as life at fish camp is exciting and brings our entire families together.

Our kayaks are very full with the addition of our fish catch. The kayak that we towed empty on the way to fish camp is now very full and almost overflowing. This is a very good thing, as we need extra fish for the upcoming potlatch. The kayak does not have much freeboard, and we need to be careful that it will not tip during our return home. It is nice that it is a downriver float with the current. We have to watch for sandbars that have appeared since our earlier journey upriver to fish camp. The water level always drops during fishing season and sandbars appear where none existed before. We do not want to hit a sandbar going downriver, as it is harder to pull a kayak from it. The current wants to push a kayak onto the sandbar.

As we approach Kagemuit, we are happy to finally be home again, especially after a very successful fishing season we experienced.

Chapter 5

Tungay returned to his home in Mamimuit. His parents had their own fish camp below his home and did not need him to bring any of the fish catch home with him.

After our return home, our attention now focused on the activities needed before the fall berry picking season began. We unloaded the fish from the kayaks and put them in barrels for storage and placed them in the smokehouse. We salted some of the fish we caught at the very end of the season that were still somewhat fresh. The salted salmon was also placed in barrels for storage. We salted fish by placing a bunch of fish in a barrel then adding a layer of salt. We continued this layering of fish and salt until the barrel was full. These barrels went into the smokehouse for storage. I especially enjoyed the salted salmon for a change in diet and taste. The salmon that were kept for the dogs were hung in the smokehouse rafters.

After fishing season and before berry picking, we needed to work on the cold storage pit. This was a hole that was dug into the permafrost which acted as a cold place to hold our berries from rotting and spoiling. The permafrost was perfect for berry storage. It was cold near the bottom. It was wide enough to hold the barrels of berries and deep enough to use the permafrost to keep them cold. We used pieces of wood to cover the opening. Each flood would require us to make necessary repairs to it. By this time of year, the flood water that entered would be gone either by evaporation or seeping into the soil from below. If we had to dig a new hole, the process would be a lengthy and physically hard one. The permafrost occurs only a few inches from the surface. Because it is permanently frozen ground, a person can only dig a few inches at a time. You dig as deep as possible, then let the sun melt more of the dirt down below. We continued this dig and melting process until we had the hole big enough for storage of our barrels. It takes many days to dig a cold storage pit. Without our cold storage pit, we would have no way to keep our berry harvest fresh. We are thankful for our permafrost that is a part of our land.

During the fall the days shorten and the temperature drops. The tundra green of summer turns red, orange, and brown this time of year. A beautiful time of year with all the varied colors. The ducks, geese, and other waterfowl that we relied upon for food and eggs would be heading south again. I did not like the fact that they had to migrate to distant lands, but if they did not migrate, they would not return next year. The newly hatched birds from early spring were now grown large enough to fly the long distance to their southern wintering grounds. The tundra was easier for walking this time of year. The summer sun dried out the soil so that we did not require tall boots as we did during the spring.

These were telltale signs that the time for berry picking was not far away. We did not need as much preparation for berry picking. We did need to take a gun, buckets, wall tent, cooking utensils, some food, and our heavy parkas, as it could get cold at night. We would spend a few days at berry camp rather than weeks at fish camp. As we departed for berry camp, Ma and Pa went in one kayak, Anngaq in one, and I in my kayak towing an empty kayak with the barrels that would hold the berries we picked. Nayagaq would stay at the cabin with Kuvak and Algaq.

Our journey to berry camp took us a little upriver and to the right to follow the Atsiyar slough. It was a day's journey following the slough to the high tundra. When the hills came into view, we knew that we were close to the good berry picking sites. We called the hills Atsaq qemiq, which means berry hills according to Pa.

As we kept kayaking toward the hills, we watched the tundra, looking for the ripening salmonberry. This was the berry we sought during this journey. As more ripe berry fields came into view, we looked for a beach that would provide easy access to the tundra where we would set up camp.

The days were beginning to shorten in the fall, and we needed to find a campsite before dark. Pa would land his kayak first and conduct a bear check of the area to determine if it really was a safe site. If Pa decided it was not a good site, then we continued looking for a better site. Once we determined a site was good for picking and safe from bears, then we unloaded the kayaks and set up the tent first. Ma would get the cooking organized and ready for eating.

Meals at berry camp usually consisted of dried fish, pilot crackers, and tea or coffee. The tea was Labrador tea picked fresh from the tundra. The water for camp came from the slough, as compared to our riverbank home that was silty and brown. After the meal was eaten and utensils cleaned, we made a campfire to just sit and talk about the berry picking day to come.

It was the salmonberry that we were after this trip, as the blueberry would be our goal during a later trip. There were also cranberries, currants, and blackberries available that we also picked to add to our variety of fruit berries. When the campfire died down, we all went to bed in preparation for a successful day of picking tomorrow.

After we shared our breakfast meal, it was time to gather our buckets and start looking for a good patch of salmonberries. The mosquitoes were a real pest this time of year, especially when there was no wind. Since it was cooler this time of year, we wore long-sleeve shirts which helped prevent some mosquito bites.

I tried to find a big, heavy patch of berries so I could just sit, pick, and fill my bucket. After a couple of days of sitting on the berry-rich tundra, my pants would begin to look the same color as a salmonberry. The size of salmonberries were much larger than blueberries, so it did not take as many to fill my bucket. While I was picking, an Arctic fox came around curious about what I was doing in his domain. He likely never saw a person before in his entire life. The mosquitoes were a bigger concern, as there were so many of them and every one of them wanted to bite me. It was very sunny with no wind, which made the situation worse. I tried my best to ignore them, but it sure was not easy.

Ma had left berry picking early so she could start our meal by the time we arrived. Pa always brought his gun along while berry picking. After we finished eating our noon meal, Pa went to the local lake to shoot a duck or goose to add to our evening meal. We hoped he would have success because I was hungry for something different to eat. Hopefully, there would be a few birds left that had not gone south. Pa came back with two ducks that he was able to shoot for our evening meal. After the meal we kept the fire going to have fresh tea that we picked from the tundra while we picked berries.

During teatime we recounted our berry picking experience. Anngaq said he had seen a bear in the distance, but it did not come his way. When the bear raised up to have a better look at him, he simply went back on all fours and went the other way. He seemed to be curious only about our presence. Pa was still a little concerned about tomorrow, especially if there was a cub nearby that Anngaq could not see in the distance. This time of year, some of the bears were eating berries from the tundra. Most bears were still eating salmon carcasses along the slough. The salmon had completed their migration to their spawning grounds and had died, leaving their carcasses on the bank of the slough.

Usually, we needed only two days of picking to fill the two barrels that we brought. We filled one and began to fill the second one with today's harvest. Tomorrow we should be able to fill the second barrel. The next day of picking was another sunny day, but with enough wind to keep the mosquitoes in the tundra and not in the air. During our picking, Ma spotted a bear that was probably the same one Anngaq saw yesterday. This time it came our direction. Ma shouted to Pa that a bear was coming. He picked up his gun and walked toward where Ma had been picking. Pa walked toward the bear and stood tall and waved his arms to try and stop its approach. The bear kept coming, so Pa shot his gun in the air, which stopped its approach. He shot again toward the bear. The bear now stopped and turned to run away. The bear realized he was not welcome and soon left the area. We continued picking but kept a careful watch for other bears. Bears this time of year wanted to pick berries to help them fatten up before their winter hibernation.

During our evening meal we decided to depart tomorrow to be safe from any more bear encounters. We would return in a few weeks to pick blueberries.

The trip home went easier as we kayaked with the current. The Atsiyar slough water came from the berry hills as it flowed toward the Kusquqvak River. Pa and Ma led the way in their kayak, so that if any ducks were still sitting in the water, he would have an opportunity to shoot. He was able to shoot three ducks during the return trip. Duck soup would taste good during our evening meal after we arrived home. Pa kept the gun with him as protection from any bear that was eating salmon carcasses along the slough.

The wind that we experienced on the tundra now created significant waves as we entered the Kusquqvak River. I had to be very careful in my kayak as I was towing the kayak that contained two full barrels of berries. The extra load caused my kayak to behave very unstably, and I had to watch the waves to navigate through them. I was somewhat concerned about my ability to keep upright. When I entered the middle of the river, the waves became larger. I took on some water as the waves splashed over the front of my kayak. If there is a supreme being, I need him now.

I kept my focus on the opposite side of the river. With each paddle I sensed that I was going to make it across. With the middle of the river behind me, I sensed the stretch of river to the opposite shore had fewer waves that were not as high. Pa's training of my kayak skills paid off, and I knew I had made it through the worst part of the river crossing.

Once I landed my kayak and the one in tow, Pa and Anngaq met me to congratulate my successful crossing. "I am very proud of the way you handled the river crossing," said Pa. I told him, "I just followed the training you taught me when I was younger about how to handle the river." I did admit there was a time during the crossing that I began to question whether I was going to make it.

With our kayaks pulled up on shore, we carried the two barrels of salmonberries to the cold storage pit. They would stay cool until we needed to use them.

Between the two berry picking seasons, we used this time to work with our fish nets to mend and repair. They were completely dry after being hung on the drying racks in the smokehouse, which made them easier for mending. During the fishing season, fish when caught would try to free themselves. Working the nets every day also would tear them over time. After we mended the nets and placed them on our drying racks for a few days, we would carefully roll them up and hang them in our smokehouse. We would need them during the winter as we used them under the ice. By the time this work was complete, we would be ready for blueberry picking.

A few weeks later we repeated our effort as we did during salmonberry picking as we journeyed back to our berry picking camp. This time we were much more aware of the presence of bears. Bears were getting ready for hibernation, but there still might be bears not ready to sleep for the winter. Now that the salmon had completed their spawning and there were few if any carcasses left in the slough, the bears were now finding the tundra berries becoming a major part of their diet.

We spent enough days picking blueberries to fill the barrels that we brought. Fortunately, we did not have any bear encounters and our time at camp was uneventful. We were happy about that because you never know how the mind of a bear works.

As we headed back to our cabin, our thoughts were consumed with grass harvest. We unloaded the barrels of blueberries and brought them to the cold storage pit. Our cold storage was now filled to capacity with both the salmonberry and blueberry barrels.

Blueberries were used in making akutaq or Eskimo ice cream and also processed into jams or syrup. The salmonberries were also used in making akutaq. I especially like salmonberries in a bowl with Carnation milk and sugar. Now that berry picking season was over, we turned our attention to grass harvest.

As fall approached, the grass we harvested eventually matured, died, and turned yellow. Once the grass turned yellow, we would begin the harvest. The best grass to harvest grew in marsh and bog areas. It needed plenty of water to grow tall. When fall came, the grass field had dried out and we could begin the harvest without getting wet. Grass harvest was a family operation. Pa and me and Anngaq used hand scythes to cut the grass and place them in bundles tied together with long blades of grass. The tied bundles were picked up by my sister Nayagaq and piled at the edge of the field. My youngest brother and sister came along and played in the uncut grass. They were so short they could hide in the tall grass. It was a game for them. I remember doing the same when I was their age. They would hide in the grass so that Nayagaq was constantly calling out to them so she could keep watch over them. Once enough bundles had been completed, we carried them to our cabin and placed them in the smokehouse to keep the grass dry. We spent days cutting as much grass as the smokehouse would hold. We used a lot of dried grass to bed the dogs and line the inside sole of our mukluk winter boots. The dogs needed the grass to keep their doghouse dry and warm during the winter. Every time Anngaq added new grass to their doghouse, they were so tail-wagging happy. It made us feel good to do something that the dogs appreciated.

Grass was used to line our winter boots. This added warmth and comfort to them. We had to replace the grass as it wore out and no longer served its purpose. The best grass blades were separated from each bundle and saved for weaving.

Ma oversaw the separation and told us which ones were to be kept. We kept them inside the cabin in a place where they would not get disturbed. She would spend the long winter nights weaving grass to make baskets, mats, and dolls. Ma learned some of her technique from her Ma and by watching grandma. She was already a good grass weaver when she married Pa. Her village where she grew up was well known for excellent basket grass weavers. My grandma still spent a lot of time grass weaving. It was this work that kept her happy and strong. Every time we went to visit her, she was working on a weaving project at the side of her bed. Every girl in the village had a grass doll that she made for them.

Since our village would be hosting the annual potlatch this winter, there was an added need to make grass weaving items that would be handed out to visitors attending the potlatch. My Ma and grandma were busier than usual making grass baskets and dolls to be handed out. The dance fans were made by both the men and women. Pa would make the handle portion of the dance fan out of grass and Ma would add feathers to decorate each one. Since both Anngaq and Nayagaq would be performing their "First Dance" this potlatch, both Pa and Ma were busy making their fans to use during their dance.

It was not only grass that we harvested during late fall, but also driftwood. Looking for driftwood was done all year long. There was added concern for driftwood during late fall before freeze-up when the river could not be counted on for travel any longer. We needed all the wood we could find for heating the cabin, cooking our meals, and the meals for the dogs. Pa, Anngaq, and I went with our kayaks upriver in search of wood. The area near the big eddy was a good place to look, as the river current caused driftwood to catch on the sandbar opposite the cut bank. We kayaked as long as it took to find enough wood to bring home. We could usually count on finding wood along the river's edge. There must be a lot of trees upriver to provide so many for us. When we found a log, we would tie a rope around it and let it float and follow behind our kayak.

Bringing the wood to shore in front of the village was just the beginning of more work—cutting it into useful pieces that would fit the cookstove and barrel kettle for cooking dog food. I cannot underestimate the great importance of finding wood. Sometimes a single large tree would be spotted floating by the front of the village. The people were alerted, and it was everyone with a kayak available to go after it and bring it to shore.

Wood was a necessity to survival in the winter. Without wood, a real chance of freezing to death was very possible. We looked in on grandpa often to make certain they had an adequate supply. To conserve our wood supply, we would let the fire go out during the night. Pa would get up first and restart the fire each morning. We kept a supply of blankets near each bed and added additional blankets during the night as the cabin began to get cold. Restarting the fire each morning felt so good to be warm again.

Chapter 6

With berry picking complete and all the other winter preparation work complete, we focus the time before freeze-up on the annual moose hunt. In the past we did not go moose hunting. After Arlunaq, my uncle, married Kiak, moose hunting became an annual rite of passage before freeze-up.

Kiak came from far upriver at the edge of Yupik and Indian country. She was half Yupik and half upriver Indian. Her village was our destination to go moose hunting. Her family maintained a moose camp near there. Because of Arlunaq's marriage to her, we were able to hunt moose in the area near her family using their camp.

Typically, Eskimos and Indians do not get along. Kiak's family was very pleasant. The upriver Indians always welcomed us when we went to visit during moose hunt. They treated us kindly. Eskimos thought all Indians were like the tundra raiders that brought death and destruction to the lower river villages. We found out that was not true. Her village people treated us with respect and kindness just like Kiak's family. Her family was always happy to see her every fall. We just came along as part of her family.

We prepared for our journey to moose camp by making a trip to Mamimuit to buy extra food, provisions, and especially ammunition for our moose hunt guns from Tagneq's store. I liked this trip as it gave me the chance to see Tungay again. He was envious of our trip to moose hunt and was disappointed that he never got to go that far upriver. Our village was as far upriver as he ever kayaked.

The journey to Kiak's home village takes three days by kayak. We take four kayaks with us. Pa, myself, and Arlunaq with Kiak in one. Pa tied one kayak to his which carried a tent and as few provisions as possible because we needed all the room possible to haul the moose meat on our return trip. During our first day out, we go past our fish camp. The next village upriver is called Kameglimiut. Cakiraq, my aunt Qavcik's husband, came from this village. We had some connection with them, but only when we went there when they hosted a potlatch. The people that live in Kameglimiut are all from the family to which Cakiraq belongs. It is a large village of seven cabins. They are all Yupik. When they host a potlatch during the winter, we travel to their village using dog teams. We stay with one of Cakiraq's relatives while we visit during the potlatch. Their communal house is much larger than ours.

As we pass the village, we observe from their full drying racks of fish that it was a very successful fishing season for them. There are a lot of barking dogs once they see us from their dog yards. The barking dogs alert the children of our presence. A large group of children stop their play long enough to wave to us and greet us shouting from the riverbank. We wave our kayak paddles to them in response as we continue our journey upriver. Once we follow the river around a bend, we lose sight of the village.

By early evening we encounter an area of the river surrounded by small hills on both sides which we call the rapids. This narrows the river and causes the flow of water to speed up considerably. The current is now so fast that we need to beach our kayaks and get out and pull them while walking on the beach. Once we can no longer maintain our speed upriver, we must simply pull them from the shore. The rapids portion of the river doesn't go very far. It is just the inconvenience of having to pull our kayaks rather than paddling.

When we can get back in our kayaks, the sun begins to set, and it is time to stop and set up camp. We are looking for a good place to anchor our kayaks and begin to unload the items we need for camp. We set up the wall tent while Kiak makes a fire. Making fire is one of her skills that she enjoys and takes pride in. She finds water from a nearby stream and begins boiling water for coffee and tea.

It becomes dark by the time the tent is pitched and the water is boiling. Arlunaq brought dried fish from his summer's salmon catch that we enjoyed along with pilot crackers and something hot to drink. After visiting around the fire and letting it die down for the night, we retire to the tent for a needed night of sleep. Just as we begin to sleep, we are listening to a pack of wolves trading howls between themselves among the surrounding hills.

We are awakened to the smell of fresh brewed coffee that Kiak started from the embers of last night's fire. Once the morning meal is finished, we take down camp and set off for a second day of kayaking.

This section of the Kusquqvak River widens and meanders through the tundra of treeless and boring environments from my perspective. No villages exist throughout this section of the river. A few abandoned cabins from long ago exist. These abandoned cabin sites represent the hopes of some settlers attempting to start a new life. They likely had thoughts of making a living in the wilderness within the new frontier. The cabins gradually sink into the tundra. The owners unknown.

The river is home to beaver and otter that greet us as curious objects as they bob up and down in the water. There are still some waterfowl that have not begun their migration south. For those ducks that just paddle in the water, they become an evening meal at the end of our gun. It is great to have duck for our evening meal.

From our kayak we see a large patch of blueberries that are still ripe. We stop and have them for a quick snack. Stopping for a few berries is a quick rest that our bodies need. We pick some to store as a snack while we paddle upriver. It is an opportunity to lay back and rest our entire body. We notice nearby a group of three cabins. They look as though they are occupied. We walk over to them, but no one is home. A few dogs are lying in the sun. Our approach wakes them up, but all they do is walk away. Near the cabins are three gardens. Some of the vegetables have been harvested, but not all. There are fish nets on drying racks, but they have been dry for a long time. Their fishing season had ended some time ago. Where are the occupants? Maybe they have gone moose hunting upriver also. No sign of any kayaks. We take our blueberries that we picked and go back to our kayaks to continue upriver.

As evening approaches, a heavy thick fog envelops us. Not sure what caused the fog, but there seems to be no reason for it to suddenly appear. We decide it is a good time to anchor our kayaks and set up camp. This portion of the tundra is dry. We don't need our tall mukluks to walk on the tundra.

A small pond nearby provides the water for Kiak to boil. This meal we have duck that Pa readies to be cooked over the fire. My appetite needs something substantial like a good, cooked duck.

While having our meal, we talk about our arrival at Kiak's village. Kiak recalls her stories of life while she was a little girl. I have heard them before but give her pleasure as though I heard them for the first time. Growing up in an upriver village among hills and tall trees is too foreign to my thinking. It all sounds so inviting, but being a downriver tundra dweller is where my heart belongs. I enjoy the wide-open expanse we experience at Kagemuit. Would I really be happy living among the trees? If I had to move, I think it would be somewhere among the treeless tundra. It has become my life, and I am well adjusted to it. I do enjoy listening to her talk about moose camp experiences. As the fire goes out, we retire to the tent for a much-needed rest and sleep from another day of paddling. Just one more day to go. As I prepare to go to sleep, my mind thinks about all my experiences I have had while growing up with a wonderful Pa that has taught me the Eskimo ways. Our large extended family at Kagemuit is so important to me. How life would be so different if they were all suddenly taken away from my life. Yes, we have just one more day to go.

As we again wake up to Kiak's good-smelling coffee, the fog has lifted, and we can see the hills in the distance. From my perspective they could be large mountains as compared to the flat terrain back home. We are assured that our destination is getting closer. I can see the excitement building in Kiak's voice as she desires so much to see her parents and other family members.

As soon as we kayak a little more upriver, the trees suddenly appear. This is such a change that is immediate. We go from tundra with no trees to land that is all trees. I always think about what causes this sudden transformation. I can't explain the feeling in words. How does this happen? The Eskimos have stories about how an animal removed all the trees from the land and suddenly had a change of heart and quit removing the trees. This is why the tundra has no trees. But grandpa and Pa do not believe those creation stories that are told. They feel deeply in their being that a supreme being designed the land the way we see it today. I believe in them and hold to their beliefs. In my heart I believe they have the real truth even if it does make us different in the minds of my uncles and aunt. This is a part of the river country that we never experienced until we started moose hunting with Kiak. It is likely that from this area and above is where our driftwood comes from that we critically need at Kagemuit.

It is fall and the hardwood tree leaves are turning colors. The yellow leaves contrast against the green of the evergreen trees. This creates a very beautiful landscape as we travel deeper into the Chagemuit region.

Being among the trees, we observe bird life very different from back home. The big black birds called ravens seem to have a remarkable intelligence. They behave more like people than birds. This trait and how they respond to their environment is likely why there are so many Eskimo and Indian stories that are told that feature them as almost human. We see many eagles either sitting at the top of the trees alone or with a nest that probably houses either eggs or little eagles. They look so regal with their mature white head and very dark bodies. They look like they should be a very important bird.

Animals the local people call squirrels are everywhere. They jump from tree to tree so agile in the way they use each tree. Some trees have what look like nests that I think belong to squirrels. They must be busy harvesting pine nuts and then bury them in the ground. It could keep a person busy just watching them. If we get too close to them with our kayaks, they will chatter loudly at us to keep our distance.

As we continue, the hills become taller and with trees that only exist at the base. The top of the large hills are barren with no trees, just rocks. Since we have been paddling for a long time on our journey today, we decide to stop and have a meal. Kiak isn't sure she wants us to stop, but she yields to our tired bodies. She is anxious to get home. Kiak starts a fire to heat water and roast our leftover duck from last night.

Birds the local people call camp robbers walk right up to us as we eat. I give them a few pieces of broken pilot crackers, and they rush to place them in their beaks and walk away to have a lunch of their own. I think you could feed them pilot crackers all day and they would continue to come begging for another new bite. The forest is also full of small red squirrels. They may be small but are not afraid of people. Rather than run away like the larger squirrels, they stand their ground and chatter loudly at us. Even when we try to provoke them by walking up to them, they only chatter louder and do not move. We have been introduced to many birds and animals that we do not have in the Kagemuit area.

I see why Kiak likes to return to this area each year. We enjoy the leftover duck and then walk to the river to continue our journey.

After a period of time, we begin to see in the far distance mountains that have snow at the top. These are the mountains that have snow all year round. They must be very tall and yet so far away. Once we see these mountains, we know that Kiak's village is close.

We start to see fishwheels that have been moved out of the river and pulled up on the beach. They are secured to the trees on the riverbank so that next year's flood does not float them down the river. Their fish season has ended and it is time to protect the fishwheels from freeze-up. We never saw a fishwheel until we began coming this far upriver. These people use fishwheels rather than gill nets to catch their salmon. Seeing the fishwheels means that we are soon to enter the village of Chagemuit.

Chagemuit is a little larger than Kagemuit as it has eight cabins that are a mix of Yupik families, many of which belong to Kiak's mother's family, and upriver Indian families which belong to Kiak's father's family. This is why Chagemuit is a mixed village, as it is situated between the downriver Yupik villages and the upriver Indian villages. The families that live here are very friendly to each other and live in harmony and help each other when needed. It is a wonderful village to visit.

As we pass by the first few cabins, we are greeted by children that were outside playing. We are complete strangers to be stared at. They don't see many kayaks at this village this far from the mouth of the river. We are not just strangers, but our kayaks are strange-looking canoes. We search for a cabin that has a large religious cross above its door. That symbol designates Kiak's parents' cabin. We beach our four kayaks in front of their cabin. The children that first saw us come running to meet us at the beach.

The noise they make causes Kiak's Pa, Tuntuvak, and Ma, Uglaniiq, to come outside and see why the children are so excited. When they recognize Kiak, they run to meet her and give a huge hug and a kiss from both. It is obvious there is a very strong bond between Kiak and her parents. They are so happy to see her after a year has passed since the last moose hunt. Eventually her other brothers and sisters come to welcome her and give her hugs. It is heartwarming to see the village still cares for her so deeply and from the heart. Her entire family gathers and decides to give us a potlatch at the communal house this evening as a welcome ceremony. The communal house is where we stay while in Chagemuit. We move our personal belongings to the communal house then walk around the village to discuss any changes we notice from our visit the year before. There is a new cabin being built for one of Kiak's nephews that married during the year. All the walls made of logs and gables are completed. Only the roof needs to be completed just in time for its first winter season. The cabins upriver are made of very fresh logs from nearby trees. Because they can use fresh felled trees, they need to have the bark removed which then reveals a very new-looking log. Our cabin logs are selected from whatever driftwood came downriver for us to use. By the time we get the logs, they are gray and old-looking without any bark. I wish we could have such fresh-looking trees for our cabin use. By the time we walk back to the communal house, people are waiting for us.

When inside, we are treated with a fine meal of moose, bear, and salmon. Akutaq and bird eggs are provided as dessert. After the meal is completed, Tuntuvak introduces us to everyone. All the families greet us warmly. In exchange for the wonderful meal we are given, we brought with us an Eskimo YoYo to give to each family. Kiak explains the YoYos are made by Arnack from stuffed grass and fur seal skin. Pa demonstrates how they are used to spin each YoYo in opposite directions. It is a fun time had by all as we watch everyone try to make them spin in opposite directions. After everyone has a chance to spin their YoYo, it is time for dancing. Each family performs a dance that reflects each family's strength and daily life. The families of Chagemuit represent a mix of Yupik and upriver Indian. I am familiar with the Yupik dance and the meaning of each action. The upriver Indian dancers are more unfamiliar to me, but I really enjoy the colorful displays and creativity in the costumes. Even the children are dressed in such a way to demonstrate their pride in their native ways. After each family performs at the potlatch, it is time for them to depart.

We are very tired and ready for sleep. We have come very far during this day and the excitement upon arrival has made us quite tired. Tomorrow, we are going to moose camp, and I am very excited about the prospects of a successful moose hunt.

After we wake up, we walk to Kiak's parents' cabin for a morning meal. Uglaniiq already has the water hot for coffee and tea and a few pancakes are ready to eat. There is maple syrup available to pour over our pancakes. They can purchase maple syrup from an upriver store that orders it for sale. The maple trees that do exist in the area do not produce the sap needed to make the syrup. After we eat our fill, it is time to prepare for moose camp.

We gather the food, guns and ammo, blankets and warm winter parkas and head for our kayaks. Tuntuvak loads his personal gear into his canoe. The people that go to moose camp are Pa, me, Arlunaq, and Tuntuvak. Kiak stays at the cabin with her Ma.

Moose camp is upriver a short distance to a slough draining into the Kusquqvak River from the north. We enter the slough and paddle for what seems a long time among the trees that make me feel closed in. The narrow slough with the tall trees so close makes me feel very uncomfortable as it is so unnatural feeling. Eventually the cabin that is our moose camp comes into view.

By my standards it is a mansion. The logs forming the walls are very large. The door is built very sturdy and heavy. Tuntuvak explains that the door needs to be that way to keep out any bear that would try to force an entry to the cabin. It has very nice windows that provide a good view to watch everything that happens outside. The inside has a big table and several chairs all made from smaller logs from the forest. There are four bunk-style beds also made from logs. In the middle of the cabin is a large cookstove. It is about the same size as the one we have in our cabin at home. Cabin life at moose camp is going to be very comfortable. No wall tent living here. After we bring our items to the cabin, we leave to survey the surrounding area for possible moose signs and activity.

The area surrounding the cabin consists of some mixed hardwoods with most of the trees being spruce, pine, and fir. There are several paths leading away from the cabin. Tuntuvak chooses the well-worn path that leads to a marsh with a small lake. It seems an ideal location to encounter a moose using the lake for water and browse. Moose signs are everywhere with evidence of moose scat and many trees showing signs of bull moose rubbing their antlers against them to wear off the velvet that covers them. The smaller trees have all their bark worn off from moose scraping their antlers against them. There are several moose trails that intersect our walking trail that all lead to the marsh and lake.

As we walk the trail, we are greeted by many chattering squirrels that do not appreciate our presence. We are intruders that need to be told to go away. There is much evidence of porcupines as many trees have bark removed from their activity. So much bark is removed by porcupines that it causes many of them to die. The trail ends at the edge of the marsh with a view of the lake. In the middle of the lake is a beaver den. From where we stand, we can see evidence of many trees that beavers have cut down to make a dam across a small stream that flows into the lake. Today they are busy applying mud to the dam with their paddle-shaped tail. There is a nonstop line of beavers coming and going from the dam repair work. The saying, "busy as a beaver" truly describes their work repairing the dam. It is easy to spot the tree stumps that once were tall trees that show the sign of their chewing to a point where the tree would fall. I always wonder how their teeth can be so strong to chew through the bark and wood. Once the tree is down in the water, they have to move the logs to where they want them to make the dam to support the force of water to pool behind. What a wonderful display of natural engineering.

A few ducks occupy the lake as they represent the stragglers that have not yet migrated south. If we had a gun, it would have tempted us to shoot a few for a nice meal. While we watch all the activity around the lake, a couple of cow moose are seen on the other side wading through the marsh to get a drink from the lake. Where there is a cow moose, there is a bull somewhere in the area as it is their mating season. Our optimism is very high that a successful hunt will be had. We will return tomorrow morning with our guns and hopefully catch a bull moose.

We turn and head back to the cabin. It is time for our evening meal. We aren't sure what Tuntuvak's wife Uglaniiq has made ahead for us to share at mealtime. It gives me an uneasy feeling walking the trail back to the cabin. I feel very closed in with the tall trees so that I can't see far ahead and to my sides as I am accustomed to while back home on the open treeless tundra where I can see forever.

As we approach the cabin, we are greeted by chattering squirrels wishing we would go away. Before we enter the cabin, I have to check on our kayaks to ease my mind that they are still anchored on the beach. I am amused to see a couple of otters swimming near them as if they are guarding our property from other animals.

As I enter the cabin, Tuntuvak is busy boiling water and heating the moose stew that Uglaniiq has prepared for us. The cookstove warms the cabin, taking the chill off the inside, so I do not need the parka that I wore outside and hang it on one of the moose tines that is nailed to a wall next to the door. The water is boiling, and I help myself to a cup of coffee. The cabin is well stocked with sugar and canned condensed milk, and I try some of both. Once the moose stew is ready, we each take our share. It is very good, and I am able to have another bowl from the leftover. Tuntuvak shares his fishing season's success. Each family's fishwheel produced more than enough fish to provide for the winter needs of people and dogs. He recalls the incident where a large driftwood log hit his younger brother's fishwheel that broke one of its baskets and paddle. It had to be pulled to shore, and a new basket rod and paddle had to be made from available spruce that they kept just in case this occurs. They are prepared for any situation that might happen. Fortunately, it occurred while the salmon run was slow, so there was no real damage to the fish catch.

When we finish our evening meal, it is getting very dark. There are oil lamps available, so we light them to provide significant light in the cabin. We use the light to clean the dishes and check our guns to be certain they are ready for tomorrow's hunt.

The morning begins with light rain with a little fog. This weather is good for hunting because the moose will be on the move rather than bedding down in the sunny heat. "We might have a good hunt," states Tuntuvak with optimism in his voice. We follow the trail we used yesterday and take up our hunting positions near the edge of the marsh overlooking the lake. The beavers are not as busy this morning. They are probably resting in their lodge from all the activity we observed yesterday.

As the light drizzle turns into light rain, we see a cow moose come out of the woods heading for the lake to get a morning drink. She is quickly followed by another cow moose. Probably the same ones we saw yesterday. At this time Tuntuvak begins rattling his moose antlers that he uses to call them close. He also at the same time makes a moose call with his voice. He also rubs them against any available tree branch to simulate a moose cleaning his antlers of velvet. Now we wait and see if there are any bull moose responding. With two cows around there must be a bull not far away.

The light rain keeps falling. I am happy we brought our rain gear with us from fishing season. While waiting for a bull to show, we are entertained by a group of beavers with little ones. The little beavers swim as fast as they can go to escape the adults that chase them just a short distance. I never observed this playful behavior from our beavers back home.

It takes a long time, but eventually Tuntuvak's antler rattling and calling brings a set of big bull moose antlers to show just above the tall grass on the side of the lake where the cows are still eating. Any type of hunting requires patience and the ability to stay focused on the work that is required to get the results that you strive for. Tuntuvak is clearly a great example of that patience. There is no giving up even when it seems as though your efforts are not leading to any results. Soon the moose comes into view with his head focused in our direction where the calling originated from Tuntuvak. Tuntuvak raises his set of antlers to show the bull that another bull moose may be in the vicinity on the opposite side of the lake from him.

Tuntuvak whispers to Pa to get ready to shoot when the bull turns sideways and offers a nice target as he walks to go around the lake and check out this competitor bull moose. The two cows belong to him, and he is not about to share them with a bull across the lake. The lake is too deep to wade across, so he has to walk around the edge of the lake to get to where we stand. Pa needs to shoot when the bull turns because he will lose his shot when the moose goes back into the forest of evergreens.

The bull does as Tuntuvak expects, and when the bull is broadside, Pa levels his gun to sight in the moose and pulls the trigger. The noise from the gun abruptly breaks the silence and echoes throughout the forest. The two cows are startled and immediately run out of the marsh and into the woods making a tremendous noise as they leave in a rush from the lake. The bull that was in Pa's sights falls immediately to the ground. It is a fatal shot that kills the bull instantly. Pa demonstrates his excellent marksmanship that I am always very impressed with—his skill that he has honed over his many years as an outdoorsman.

We gather our scabbards that each of us brought to carry the cut-up moose back to camp and start to walk around the lake to where the moose fell. There is a well-worn animal trail that follows the edge of the lake. It makes our walk very easy. Everyone is very happy about a successful hunt. Pa acknowledges Tuntuvak's skill at calling moose. The moose was killed around mid-afternoon so there is plenty of time to cut it up before darkness falls. The light rain has stopped but it is still cool so that will help keep the meat chilled. After walking halfway around the lake to the opposite side, we come to the bull moose laying in the marsh grass. The antlers are very large to indicate that it is a mature moose. Everyone takes out their knives and begins cutting up the moose. Tuntuvak is very precise and expedient in his instructions to us as to the procedure required for each cut to maximize our effort and keep the meat intact. This moose will provide plenty of meat for our family during the winter when we desire food other than fish. There is also enough to share with others in the village. Grandpa and grandma will be very excited to get a portion of the meat. It is almost dark when we finish skinning and cutting it into quarters that we can carry back to the cabin.

We arrive at camp and help Tuntuvak lift the moose meat up into the cache that his grandpa had built years ago when he first used the cabin for moose hunting. It is still in good condition. It was built about sixteen feet above the ground to keep the bears from taking the meat. We carry each section up the wooden ladder to the cache door.

Once all the moose meat is stored, the door is closed and latched. The wooden ladder is laid up against a nearby tree. Hopefully our meat is safe from any animal wanting a free meal.

When that work is completed, we are ready for the evening meal. I wonder what Uglaniiq prepared for us this evening to eat. With the fire started in the cookstove and the water boiling, I volunteer to go to the underground storage and bring back another pot. I open it wondering what it contains. It is a complete roasted duck. All that we need to do is put it on the cookstove to warm it up. It is very tasty. I cannot identify what she added to make it so flavorful. After the meal we all go to bed as we are very tired from the hunt and all the work to bring the meat to the cache. Tomorrow we will try to get Arlunaq a moose for his extended family back in Kagemuit.

The next morning brings a clear sky, but it became quite cold during the night. A clear night usually allows the cold to develop. We start a fire just to keep warm as we awake for another day of hunting. The cold night is welcome as it keeps the meat chilled. Tuntuvak goes to the cold storage and brings back a jar of sourdough starter to make pancakes for the morning meal. Tuntuvak adds flour and water then makes some great-tasting sourdough pancakes. As soon as we clean the dishes and check our guns, we are ready to set out for another day of hunting.

It is cold enough to wear our parkas, fur cap, and mittens. As Tuntuvak opens the cabin door and walks toward the trail, he suddenly stops and whispers to Arlunaq, "There is a bull moose just down the trail." "I can't believe it," says Arlunaq in a startled and unbelievable voice. It is hard to believe, but there it is right in the trail ready to be shot. It is another large bull moose with very large antlers. It will be another prize catch. Arlunaq walks to the corner of the cabin and steadies his gun on the corner of the cabin wall and pulls the trigger. He kills his moose without even taking ten steps from the cabin. "I can't believe how easy this was to kill my moose," Arlunaq says in complete disbelief. "How can you be so lucky," says Pa. We each grab our knives and begin working up the moose.

It doesn't take long to complete the work of butchering the moose. There is still most of the day left so we decide to go ahead and load all the meat into the kayaks and head back to Chagemuit. We will get there before evening since we will paddle with the current the whole trip, making it a much faster trip.

As we approach the village, we are greeted by all the children. Their noise catches the attention of Kiak and her Ma. They know it has to be our return from moose camp. Kiak is very happy for another moose to add to their diet during the winter. She remarks, "Another set of moose antlers to hang on our cabin wall."

This evening, we are treated to fresh moose tongue soup prepared by Uglaniiq. It tastes very good, and I even request if I can have another bowl. It is amusing to listen to Arlunaq explain the easy moose hunt he had. Kiak remarks, "That is a little hard to believe, but I will take moose meat however you catch it." After the evening meal is finished and the dishes washed, we walk to the communal house and prepare for bedtime. It is another day of hard work, but very satisfying. It is great to have another successful moose hunt. Tomorrow, we prepare to begin our journey back to Kagemuit. It will be nice to be back home.

The next morning, we are treated to a nice morning meal prepared by Uglaniiq. After making ready to depart Kiak's home village, we are escorted to our kayaks by all the children and family members. Kiak says her goodbyes to Tuntuvak and Uglaniiq with long hugs and tears shared by both. Tuntuvak congratulates Arlunaq on a productive hunt. Pa and I exchange handshakes with Tuntuvak and thank him for his hospitality and a great hunting experience. We thank Uglaniiq for all the tasty meals she provided in her home and during our moose hunt.

We shove off in our four kayaks with one in tow full of fresh moose meat. The children run down to the beach and all of them wave to us as we head downriver. As we make our turn in the river, we see the last of them still waving to us. It is nice to no longer have to paddle against the current but just float and let the current move us down the river. We fall into an easy rhythm of paddling. It is nice to be heading home with our moose meat.

The trees that during our journey upriver looked so yellow have now lost their beautiful yellow leaves and are now barren looking. They are ready for their long winter without leaves. By the same token, the tundra that gave us so many colors of red, yellow, and brown have now lost their leaves and are now barren looking. Winter is surely just around the corner. Each morning the cold is deepening as we awaken with frosty breath and the morning fire is very welcomed.

It took three days of paddling upriver. We estimate it will take only two days to make the trip going downriver. The trip is uneventful the whole way, and on the evening of the second day we beach our kayaks in front of my cabin in Kagemuit.

Chapter 7

The moose hunt was very successful with two large bulls taken. The meat will provide us with a variety of food for our diet. We shared the meat with my grandpa and grandma. They were very excited to receive it.

The moose hide was quickly taken by Ma. She enjoys sewing them into parkas for her family members. This requires Pa to prepare it for tanning. He removes all the fat, sinew, and other matter that will keep it from tanning properly. After he removes the unwanted matter, he ties it between slats that he has bent just for this work. Once it is tanned to the point it is pliable and workable, Pa gives it to Ma for her to make whatever she needs.

Her moose hide parkas are very high quality. She also makes mittens and mukluks from the moose hides. Most families that live this far downriver do not have access to moose hide, so they make their clothing from seal skin. As a result, Ma's clothing is most unique in this part of the Kusquqvak River. With the upcoming potlatch this winter, she will make many YoYos to be given away during that event. Her moose YoYos are very desired by people as they are so unique—she decorates them with her beadwork.

The period after our moose hunt and prior to freeze-up is a busy time to make preparations for the coming winter. A family must be prepared for when winter comes. Once the cold and snow arrive, it is too late to prepare.

It is time to look over our cabin. We examine the outside cabin walls to look for areas that could allow cold weather to enter. The winter winds seem to find every tiny crack that we can't see with our eyes. Since freeze-up hasn't come yet, we are able to make mud from dirt and chink any cracks that we see. Over time the mud between the logs wears out and needs to be replaced. We look at our roof and replace any sod that has worn and lost its ability to hold and repel the rain and melting snow. We also look over grandpa's cabin and make any repairs that are needed.

During the last days before freeze-up, we take our kayaks and look for more driftwood. Searching for wood takes on a sense of most urgency now that we don't know when our last day to use our kayak will end. Once the river begins to form ice, it is too risky to be out on it in a kayak. Hitting any floating ice will easily puncture the covering of a kayak and sink it quickly. We were able to find a lot of driftwood during each of our outings. We feel confident that we have a good supply for the winter. If we do run low, we can use our dog sleds and search for wood. While the weather is good, we cut and split wood every chance we get. The wood we need is not just for my family, but for grandma and grandpa, and anyone else in the village that needs more.

We make any repairs to our kayaks. Since they are used often, there is a need to replace structural members that just wear out with age. Pa is very good at bending wood, so he can duplicate the size and bend of any piece of wood that needs to be replaced. Pa is well known for his wood-bending skills, so he is asked often for repairs or replacement wood parts from other family members. When the ice begins to form on the river, our kayaking days are over and we pull them up near the cabin and tie them to the drying racks to keep them away from the snow that will come. Now that the kayaks are stored for the winter, we turn our attention to the upkeep of our dog sleds.

Pa is in the final steps of building a new sled for trapping season. His sled was the oldest one he built for the family. We have four sleds among our family members. Pa has the oldest one, then one for me, Anngaq, and even my sister, Nayagaq, has one. Although he made repairs to it each season, it was just getting old and needed to be replaced. Regarding his new sled he is building, all that needed to be done to make it ready for use were the basket cross members. They did not need to be bent, so it would be complete soon. Just in time for a new trapping season. It certainly had that new look. It was a beautiful sled to look at. With Pa's sled-building ability, he was asked to build both complete sleds for people and make repairs to others. Sometimes Tagneq requested Pa to build a sled when he could not keep up with the orders that he received at his Mamimuit store. That worked out well for us as we could trade the newly built sleds for store purchases. Pa let me build my sled with his help. I wanted to be able to build one myself when I no longer have Pa available to show me how it was done. Dogsleds were critical to travel during the winter. We are not able to go long distances without the dogs and our sleds. Running a trapline would not be possible without them.

Just as we relied on our dogsled and dog team for long-distance travel, snowshoes were required for walking over the deep snow. Every member of my family had a pair. Large ones for adults down to small ones for my younger brother and sister. Snowshoes are needed to walk on the snow when it becomes several feet deep, especially when it hasn't been walked on during the winter. When we go out on the tundra, the need for them is required. Without a pair of snowshoes, walking on the open tundra is not possible. Too much is required of our bodies to make walking possible. Since Pa was good at wood bending, he made all our snowshoes and for many of the other families in the village. It was a part of our travel equipment to have a pair in the dogsled for each person. You did not want to get stranded outdoors without a pair available for immediate use. Snowshoes required maintenance as they aged, and the webbing loosened over time. I learned from Pa how to make the webbing and tie it to the frame. I was responsible for making sure they were ready to use before the snow fell.

The traps we used along the trapline needed to be cleaned and boiled to make them free of any scent. We checked them to make certain the trap mechanism was working as required. Over the years of use they rust, but as long as they work, the rust actually was a good thing to keep the outside scent from the trap.

Pa took over the traplines used by Apak, my grandpa. It included two traplines. One trapline was located to the west of the village. We would take the Kagemuit slough westward to the confluence of the Kapkaanaq slough that heads north to what we called the trapline hills. It was a good trapline, but a second trapline is needed because of the number of furs required for trade and sewing. The second trapline is located across the river from the island that exists in front of the village. It was also a good one with its furs being a little better quality. This trapline is located further north than the west trapline, as it went in the direction of our berry picking camp. Trapping in the winter was very important to our subsistence existence as it gave us clothing and trade opportunities.

It is during this late fall season that we made our last kayak trip to Mamimuit to trade for our winter food and provisions. We used this trip to purchase food, bending wood, traps, chain for the traps, and finally, matches for starting fire. We can't run out of those. Everyone could start a fire using flint and a knife, but it saved much time to use a match. This trip was always weather permitting. We cannot get caught in a late season storm or a sudden river freeze-up.

During this time of year, the teachers return for another school year. They took the steamship to Mamimuit then rode in the Northern Commercial Company supply boat to Kagemuit. Everyone was excited to see who returned for another year of teaching. It is unusual to have a teacher repeat two years in a row. There were always new teachers each year. Our school only taught six grades, so only two or three teachers were required. Each one was stared upon as they walked off the supply boat to give us our first impression of the person willing to teach us.

As each one came onto shore, we would greet them and assist with their belongings that they brought. It became an annual event that we looked forward to as a whole village. Tonight, there will be a potlatch to welcome our newcomers. At the potlatch we get the opportunity to visit each new teacher and learn from where they came from. Robert came from the state of Idaho. Emily came from Washington and Janet came from Oregon. Emily also worked as our village nurse. Each one gave a brief talk about their life before they came to our village. The parents introduced their children that were of school age.

At the conclusion of all the introductions, we sat down to eat our potlatch meal. We served them all aspects of our native foods. I am not certain how each one regarded our foods. We got some ideas from their facial expressions as they tried each one. We got an idea of their favorite food choices as we watched the crates of provisions being unloaded from the supply boat. Each crate represented what we call "white man's" food. After mealtime, each family performed a native dance that they had prepared just for the teacher potlatch.

After the potlatch ended, the teachers were able to have their quiet time together. I wondered about what their first impressions of our village that would become their home for the next school year were. We would do our best to make each teacher feel welcome and make them a part of our village. I looked forward to becoming friends with Robert and showing him our native ways. I will get him involved in some of my outdoor activities.

Just as Mother Nature always promises, freeze-up arrives. The temperature drops and the river begins to develop skim ice near the shore. Now is the time to pull the kayaks to the cabin if they have not already done so. Each day more ice forms toward the middle of the river and thickens. We begin to see larger chunks floating in the middle from upriver. Since it is colder up north, the ice breaks and creates these icebergs that float by. These ice chunks along with lower temperatures begin to freeze the water. As what seems an overnight creation, we awaken to a river that is completely frozen from shore to shore.

We must wait for the ice to thicken before we can walk or travel on it. A walking stick or ayaruq is used to determine whether it is safe to go out on the ice. Pa used an ayaruq whenever he walked onto the ice to use it to determine how thick the ice is. The last thing a person walking on the ice wants is falling through. As the ice is forming, there is no way to know its depth. Only a walking stick can give a person comfort that it is safe for walking.

An ayaruq was like "wise words" spoken by elders, as both gave our life guidance. Pa would not be without his walking stick when uncertain about the conditions he was going to enter. It was a necessary survival tool. It gives guidance to our lives when we do not know which way to go. It gave you guidance so you will not walk down the wrong path. According to Pa, a properly used ayaruq would lead you on the right path. A walking stick gave Pa insights as to the two paths in life—the right or the wrong one. It was up to the user of the ayaruq to choose wisely. Only after Pa, our village elder, approved that the ice was safe did we venture out on the frozen river.

The first snow was never predictable. It might occur before freeze-up, during it, or after freeze-up. One thing was certain and that was that it would come. Once the snow depth allowed, we could use our dog sleds. The sled dogs loved this time of year. This is what they are bred to do—pull a sled and go as fast as possible.

Our sled dogs are malamutes. They are large and powerful. Their fur is very thick and long. This is why they like this time of year the most. The colder the temperature, the more they enjoy this time of year. They don't like the summer as much. They are perfect for the winter travel needed to run the trapline. They are like family, and we treated them with that respect. Pa learned his dog handling skills from grandpa. I wanted to learn how to handle dogs just like Pa. Anngaq liked working with the dogs as he fed them and kept each doghouse clean and in comfortable condition.

Once the snow was deep enough, we hitched them to the sled and took them for training runs for conditioning and training to run as a team. They must be ready for the long runs required for the trapline. The position of each dog in the team is also being evaluated. Possibly a change in position is required within the team as each dog ages and matures and a change is required. We also focused on the dogs' discipline in starting and stopping. They needed to obey our commands without exception. There are too many stories of a runaway sled without a driver. That results in a very dangerous situation if caught on the tundra without a dog team and sled. Without a sled we no longer had access to our snowshoes, which are critical in a situation like this. We needed the dogs to obey our commands.

With freeze-up complete and plenty of snow on the ground, it is time to prepare ourselves for running the trapline and get the trapping season underway.

Chapter 8

Now that there is plenty of snow on the ground and the river is frozen to allow sled dog traffic, Tungay from Mamimuit has arrived. He came with his dog sled and dog team to help us with our trapping season. Every winter he comes to assist with our trapping duties as he is very skilled at trapping and snaring fur animals. Since he is one of my best friends, I looked forward to his arrival.

During the winter his Pa's store in Mamimuit is not very busy, so it is a good time for Tungay to leave and spend the winter with us. He brings provisions for our home since he will be living in our cabin with us all winter. He always remembers my Ma and Pa with a special gift from his Ma and Pa. They look forward to the surprises that he brings to them. He brought a very heavy wool sweater for Pa and a very decorated wool blanket for Ma. They will certainly use them during the long, cold winter nights. He brought a pair of heavy and warm mittens that wear all the way to the elbow for Anngaq. He said it would make preparing the boiled dog food easier and safer from the possibility of scalding his hands. Anngaq replied, "I will not admit how many times I burned myself while cooking dog food. These mittens will keep my hands safe during cooking the dog food." For Nayagaq, he brought a beaded barrette to keep her hair in place. "Now I can keep my long black hair out of the cooking food while I help Ma," Nayagaq replied with a big hug to Tungay. He brought a toy boat for Kuvak and a doll for Algaq. The entire cabin was full of excitement and appreciation for everything he brought. It was a Christmas-like atmosphere as he emptied all the items from the bag and handed them out to everyone.

Outside in his dogsled was a full winter supply of fish for his dogs and some extra for our dog team. Since he comes every winter, his dog yard is behind our cabin along with a shed to house his sled, dog harnesses, and tow line. His supply of fish went into the shed also. He uses ten dogs just like us. His dogs were not all malamutes, but a cross of dog breeds that looked more like a team that would be seen at a dog race. His dogs were bred for speed and long-distance running.

When he first arrives at the village, the presence of his dogs makes our dogs bark and howl. It will take a few days for all the dogs to realize they all belong together. All it takes is for one dog to bark and they all start barking. Until they settle into their new arrangement, it can result in very noisy days and nights. In a short time, they realize they know each other and become dog buddies.

Every family in the village has a dog team. Dog teams are essential to being able to travel in the winter. The dogs are just an extension of each family. They are treated as another member of the family. When puppies are born there is excitement as if a new baby arrives. The puppies are so much fun to play with and watch them act like the newest members of the human family. The village children come to see the puppies and cannot resist playing with them. New puppies bring the entire village together.

Having a dog team also requires that every member of the family play a part in the upkeep of the team. Pa made dog harnesses for each dog. He makes them out of the webbing that he purchased from the Northern Commercial store. Ma is responsible for making booties for each dog. She uses the leftover moose hide to stitch them together. It requires her to make many booties as they wear out and need to be replaced. Booties for dogs are as important as mukluks are for our feet. They keep the dogs' feet warm and ice-free. Anngaq makes sure each dog is comfortable and well-fed.

Before each run, Pa harnesses each dog by attaching them to the tow rope. We also tie the sled to the smokehouse with a very strong rope. It had to be tied securely as the dogs are so full of energy before each run. A very strong rope tied to an immovable smokehouse is required to hold them back. They are always ready to go. Once all the dogs are tied to the tow rope, they begin jumping and barking to let us know that they are ready to go. I would ride in the sled basket covered with a tarp to keep the cold out. When we are ready to depart, we untie the rope and off we go. Tungay will follow soon after with his dog team. They want to run fast at the start, so Pa will keep his foot on the brake to slow the team down. Eventually the team will slow into a steady tempo pace.

To head to our west trapline, we follow the Kagemuit slough to where the Kapkaanaq slough enters. This leads us north toward Nerqik qemiq or what we call in English the trapline hills. We head towards the land of trees and leave the tundra behind. This is our trapline destination.

As we enter our trapline region, we look for a good opportunity to catch fur. When we locate one, we stop the sled and put on our snowshoes and walk to the location. If it looks good for rabbits, we set up a snare where we find rabbit tracks, especially if heavily used.

If a trail looks good for fox, lynx, or wolf, we set up a leghold trap. We tie the trap to a nearby tree so the animal will not carry it away. We continue this stop-and-go routine until we use all our traps and snares. Tungay takes his sled and follows the alternate route to Nerqik qemiq and sets his snares and traps. With Tungay helping, we are well organized to get a good supply of furs. He is very skilled in placing snares and traps in the right place to be successful.

After we set all our snares and traps, we head back home. When we come upon the place where our traplines intersect, we stop and wait for Tungay if he has not already stopped and is waiting for us. We want to make certain neither of us is left on the trail overnight. Now that we have met up, we together run our sleds back to Kagemuit.

The next day we take our sleds and go across the river and take Atsiyar slough up to a junction with Pekeryaq slough that leads to a point where the tundra ends and the trees begin. Tungay takes an alternate route that he uses as his trapline. We look for good snare and trapping opportunities. The traplines on the other side of the river lead further north and as a result the furs are better quality because they are thicker and longer fur. Like yesterday, when we find a good site with plenty of tracks, we place a snare or trap. We continue this until we reach the end of our trapline. With all our snares and traps set, we head back to the location where Tungay left the trail and wait for each other.

By the time we make our turnaround on the trapline, the dogs have assumed a steady pace whereby they can run forever. It is a quiet trip back home. It is starting to get dark as we meet with Tungay. Whenever it snows while out on the trapline, it is a magical experience. The fresh snow diminishes the noise of the sled and dogs make less noise. I think dogs like the new falling snow also. It makes everything around us so quiet and peaceful.

As we return home, we each do our task of taking care of the dogs. We take each harness off the dogs and roll up the tow line. Each dog is led back to its doghouse. By this time Anngaq is cooking the dog food. Nayagaq helps with stirring the dog soup of fish while Anngaq makes the doghouses comfortable with new grass inside. When all the work is finished, we go inside and have the evening meal that Arnack has prepared.

We discuss with Tungay his prospects for his portion of the trapline. He thinks his traplines should be very productive from his observations of the animal tracks. He states that the rabbit snares should yield many rabbit skins this year. He is not as optimistic with his traps for fox, lynx, and wolf, but says it should be good, just not excellent. We tell him the northern trapline across the river looks better than the one near the Nerqik hills.

During the days we are not running the trapline, we spend our time winter fishing. The next morning, we decide to go fishing on the river.

We plan to take the fishing net and go to the Kusquqvak River and try to catch some sheefish, whitefish, pike, or burbot. We take our net setting pole, ice picks, and a net from the smokehouse and load them into the sled. After hitching up the dogs, we head down to the river. The best location for setting up our net is just above the village heading toward the big eddy.

Once we find a good site, we stop the sled and unload the net, picks, and pole. The dogs, not sure about what is going to happen next, simply lay down on the snow-covered ice and rest. We start chipping a hole in the ice big enough to maneuver the net with Tungay chipping another hole at a distance equal to the length of the ice pole. I alternate my help between Pa and Tungay. Using an ice pick to cut a hole at least two feet wide and about one to three feet deep depending upon the time of season. It is hard work and takes a long time. A series of these holes are dug the length of our net. It takes all three of us to use the ice pole to guide the net under the ice and capture it from the nearby hole. This process is repeated until the entire net is under the ice. With both ends anchored on the surface of the ice, our work is done, and we head back home. Tomorrow we will return to check the net.

As we eat our morning meal, we discuss the prospects of what the nets will yield when we check them. There is heavy snow falling with a light wind. The sun will not rise for a while, so we hope the snow and wind will diminish with the sunrise. We spend our time inside the cabin watching Kuvak pretend he is driving his toy boat across the cabin floor. Algaq shows us the new outfits that Arnack had made for the doll Tungay had given her. Arnack used some of the moose hide pieces that she had accumulated to make a small parka for the doll.

When the sun did rise near noontime, we noticed the snowfall had let up a little bit and the wind had gone down. As we opened the cabin door, we saw about four inches of new dry snow had fallen during the night. The sled had a new load of snow. It was a good decision to take the ice pick and net pole to the smokehouse yesterday after we arrived at the cabin. If we left them outside, they would have been lost in the snow. The new snow on the ground along with the light falling snow creates a quiet feeling outside.

The dogs sense that we are going to use the sled, and they begin their usual jumping and barking. As we approach the portion of the river where we set the net yesterday, we notice that the net holes have not frozen over. It snowed all night, and the new snow provided enough insulation to keep the net holes open and not frozen over. We do not have to open each hole with our ice picks. Because the holes are open, we can get right to pulling the net through the ice. There is not much resistance from the net, so we know our catch will be small. The net yields thirteen fish total. We catch six sheefish, four whitefish, two burbot, and one pike. It is less than we desire but will give us several meals other than the usual salmon. We reset the net under the ice and take the sled home with our catch of fish.

Arnack is waiting for us from the open cabin door. She is a little disappointed but happy that we did catch a few fish. She happily takes the fish and begins cutting them on the snow-covered fish cutting table next to the smokehouse. It continues to snow the whole time we are outside. Our parkas are covered in snow, especially on our hoods. The dogs are also covered in snow as the malamute heavy fur doesn't allow their body heat to melt it.

It is good to have fresh fish for our evening meal. The fish not used in our meal are placed in the underground storage for later use. Our after-meal talk includes what might be the fur harvest from the traplines. By the time we go to sleep, the snow has stopped falling. The fresh snow will give us a good idea of our trap locations.

The morning offers us clear skies but cold temperatures. Our malamute sled dogs love the cold weather. As we leave the cabin, they know we are going to visit the trapline. They start jumping and barking in anticipation of harnessing up to the sled. We take the trapline route that leads to the Nerqik hills. Tungay and Pa and I separate just above the Kapkaanaq slough to visit the traplines. At each snare and trap we stop the sled and visit each site hoping to find a catch. The rabbit snares give us about a quarter successful catch. That is normal for this early in the season. The traps give us three foxes and one lynx. A good result for this early in the season. The wolves usually trap later in the season.

As we return from our trapline, we wait for Tungay to arrive with his sled and discuss his results. We wait a considerable time for Tungay to arrive. Had he been involved in an accident? Was his trapline very successful and making him longer than usual to complete checking his snares and traps? After a long wait, he finally arrives. We see that his sled is very full of rabbits. His snares proved very successful. "Almost every snare caught a rabbit," he says. The traps only caught one fox. We are returning with many rabbits. They not only provide furs for Arnack to sew but also food for our meals. It is a very good day on the traplines. A good start to a young trapping season.

Tomorrow, we are going to our Pekeryaq traplines. When we set the snares and traps earlier, we think the Pekeryaq traplines should yield better. It would be great if our assumptions are correct.

The morning sky is cloudy, so it keeps it not as cold as yesterday morning. As expected, the dogs are excited to be taken on another trapline run. We both take off toward the river and follow the slough to the Pekeryaq slough where we go to our separate traplines. The farther we go, the deeper the snow becomes. There is much more snow on this side of the river. It must have received high winds as there are fallen trees throughout the forest that we did not observe when we ran the trapline earlier.

Our earlier prediction of a productive trapline is proving true as most snares catch rabbits and our traps so far catch two lynx and three fox. As we enter the last quarter of the trapline, we are encouraged with the catch so far. The dogs now run at a steady pace and because of the deep snow on the ground are very quiet. As we round a turn in the trail, I see the lead dog jump over a fallen tree in the middle of the trail. I yell to Pa, "There is a tree in the trail, stop the dogs!" It is too late to stop even though Pa drops the brake anchor to try and stop the sled. We hit the fallen tree, and I am thrown out of the sled as it falls on its side. Pa loses his grip on the handle and falls backward off the sled. We both watch the dogs continue down the trail dragging the sled that is now laying on its side. We yell at the dogs to stop, but they keep on going, even picking up speed with the lighter load on the sled.

There we stand in the middle of the trail with the dog team nowhere to be seen. All the furs have been tossed from the sled, so we make a pile of them to return and gather them later. Our only option is to follow the runaway sled and hope the dogs eventually stop or are stopped by the sled anchor or the sled itself. I ask Pa if he is hurt. He rubs his shoulders with some pain in his face and says, "My shoulder hurts a little when I fell and hit a tree." Pa asks how I feel, and I reply, "I feel like I have bruises all over my body." We both walk with aches and sore muscles as we do not know how far we have to walk before we will find the dog team. Pa thinks eventually either the sled or the brake anchor will catch on a tree and stop the dogs. Thankfully it only takes a short walk to find the dogs as we do not have our snowshoes to make walking easy. They are still in the sled. Just as Pa thought, the brake anchor has wound itself around a tree. The dogs are laying on the trail waiting for us to rescue them. We examine the condition of the sled. One front runner has a significant crack caused by the impact with the fallen tree. We are able to use it, but it will need replacing when we get back to the cabin. Pa's newly built sled has suffered its first accident and will require repairs.

We are almost to the point in the trail where we will meet Tungay at the meeting point. Tungay is waiting for us and sees the damage to our sled. He asks, "What happened to your sled?" We tell him the whole story of events. We tell him we will need to come back tomorrow and recover the furs that we piled on the side of the trail.

Tungay's trapline was very productive with many rabbits, foxes, lynx, and even one wolf. His prediction proved correct and even better than he expected. I ride back in Tungay's sled to keep the weight off Pa's broken sled. We do not want to make the crack grow bigger than it already is. Once back at the cabin, we have to repeat the series of events to everyone. Ma, in her stern voice, says, "There will be no sledding for you two tomorrow." She orders us to stay in the cabin to rest. Our body language with some pain tells her that we both agree with her.

The next morning Tungay and Anngaq leave to pick up the furs that we left on the trail from the accident. They take a saw to remove the fallen tree. We do not want to hit it again.

Ma allows Pa and I to skin the animals that Tungay had caught the day before. While we are outside skinning, Tungay and Anngaq return with the furs that we left on the trail. We are fortunate that the furs were not found by other animals in the woods and eaten as a free meal. They also bring back some of the tree that they cut and place in the sled. Finding firewood is a staple that can't be left behind. Our combined catch of furs during our first trapline run far exceeds our expectations. A great beginning to what we hope will be a strong trapping season.

After we skin all the catch, Pa and I have to return to the cabin under Ma's orders to rest. Ma is always correct as all of us have had a busy last few days. Tomorrow, Pa will begin repairing his sled, Tungay and I will set fish traps in the slough, and Anngaq will go back to school.

We look forward to trapping fish in the Kagemuit slough. The black fish is our target when we use fish traps in the slough. They are black in color with very tasty white meat on the inside. They are a real treat when Ma cooks them. We hope for a good fishing trip. After our evening meal and bedtime is upon us, we dream of black fish for the evening meal tomorrow.

When we awake the next morning, Pa has the cookstove fire going. Hot water is boiling for coffee or tea and Ma is busy making pancakes. After the meal, Pa begins to repair his sled. He keeps it in the cabin, and with the water still hot, Pa uses his bending pipe to shape the wood to match the runner that needs to be replaced. Tungay and I take three fish traps from the smokehouse and load them into Tungay's sled. He wants to drive his team today. I get into the sled basket and off we go toward the slough. We drop down into the bank of the slough and head west up the slough. We travel up to where the Kagemuit slough widens and we stop the sled. Tungay grabs one ice pick, and I grab the other. We begin the process of chipping a hole in the ice large enough to lower the fish trap. Chipping a hole in the ice large enough for the trap requires a lot of patience and physical strength and endurance. Pa taught me that every chip of the ice will eventually get the hole dug. I must be patient.

Pa made our fish traps. To make a fish trap, Pa looks for long, straight sapling trees. He peels the bark to expose the white wood underneath. This wood works best because it is soft and very bendable without heating it first. There are three sections to the trap. As a fish enters the trap, it must swim through the sections until it cannot go any farther. Each section is made smaller, so once a fish passes through all the sections, it can't escape. It is now caught in the trap. A door is made into the end of the trap to allow the fish to be emptied when placed on the ice.

As soon as the hole is big enough to lower the trap through it, we do so. It is cold, and if we wait too long, the hole will ice over quickly. We lower the trap to the bottom of the slough and drive a heavy wooden pole in the ice to anchor the trap. Both of us work on the third hole to make the work go faster. With all three traps in the water and anchored, we head back home. We will return later today and check the traps.

The black fish is about seven inches in length. They are elongated with a dark brown coloration. They have a white belly, and the fins have reddish-brown speckles. They are found in tundra sloughs. They are a very hardy fish. They survive the winter by moving to deep water when ice develops. They have large gills protected by gill covers that help them survive the harsh winters when they bury themselves into the bottom mud. We only catch black fish in the winter under the ice in traps. It is their white meat that we savor when cooked.

When we return to the cabin, Pa has made the necessary wood bend to replace the broken runner. He will let it shape during the night and replace it tomorrow. Nayagaq is preparing dough to make bread. She is good at breadmaking. We will look forward to having it fresh when we return from checking the fish traps. Anngaq is preparing the dogs for our next sled trip to check the traps. When he enters the cabin and tells us the dogs are ready to go, we get ourselves dressed for the weather and head to the sled. As we depart, Anngaq tells us to have a good trip and bring back a lot of black fish for our evening meal.

When we see our wooden poles stuck in the ice, we stop the sled and begin picking a hole in the ice again as it has frozen over since morning. The ice is not as thick this time, so it does not take as long to make the hole big enough to lift the trap from the water. It is an exciting time when we lift the trap out of the water because it is so full of the little black fish making a commotion as we lay it on the ice. We move on to the next traps and lay them all on the ice. We empty the fish into gunnysacks. Everyone will be happy to see our catch when we bring them home.

As we reach our cabin, everyone is waiting at the cabin door to see how many black fish we caught. Ma remarks that she is happy with our catch. She empties the fish into a large pot on top of the cookstove and begins to boil them. As we enter the cabin, we can smell the bread that has been freshly baked by Nayagaq. Our evening meal is going to be very tasty with fresh caught black fish and fresh bread.

We thank Nayagaq for the fresh bread. We don't have it very often. Just on special occasions. It is a wonderful meal of black fish, fresh bread, and tea. This makes for a very special Eskimo-style meal that the entire family enjoys. Pa thanks Tungay and me for the abundance of fish.

The next morning, we are awakened by the sound of a very windy and heavy snow blizzard outside. The cabin fire had gone out and Pa is restarting the fire in the cookstove. It is cold in the cabin, and I use every blanket to try and keep warm. We are going to be confined to our cabin for at least all day, I think. It is a whiteout blizzard, and no one wants to be outside. Not only is it extremely cold, but the blowing snow makes any outside activity impossible. A person cannot see anything in front of your face. We would get completely disoriented even trying to walk to grandpa's cabin that is very close by.

This gives Pa the time to complete his dog sled runner. With a new runner now attached to his sled, he is ready to use it again. Ma takes this opportunity to wash clothes. She uses a washboard with a bar of soap in a bucket of hot water to scrub each article of clothing. It is physical work. I am impressed with how strong Ma proves to be. Even though a blizzard rages outside, she knows this is a good time to hang the clothes outside. The blizzard will freeze the clothes so the water will bead on the clothing. This allows the wind to blow off the water beads and dry the clothes naturally. When she re-enters the cabin, she is cold and completely covered with snow. "I got the clothes washed and ready to dry," she says as a job well done. Anngaq sits in the corner of the cabin and reads a book that his teacher, Robert, had given him. He is Robert's favorite student. Robert is always giving him books to read. I also like Robert; he is a good person.

By evening mealtime the blizzard has diminished to just a light snowfall. Tomorrow morning it will be interesting to see how large the snow drifts are that were created by the high winds. Every blizzard changes the snowy landscape of the village. If items were not anchored down, they are probably blown into the tundra.

The morning brings clear skies and the usual very cold temperatures. When we open the cabin door, the snow has packed against it up to three-quarters of its height. We use the shovels that we keep in the cabin to dig ourselves out of our cabin. There is a huge snowdrift that runs the entire length of our cabin front. We next focus our attention on the dogs. Each doghouse is completely buried in snow. The dogs do not care about the situation at all. They are cozy warm inside. We walk over to grandpa's cabin to dig them out as their front door is also completely buried in snow. They certainly need our help to get out of their cabin.

The rest of the winter we fall into a routine of running the trapline, net fishing in the river, trap fishing in the slough, and going on hunting trips to catch rabbits and birds with our guns. Finding food is our top priority. Kagemuit will host the annual potlatch this year and we need extra food for that festival. Every family participates in the potlatch preparation. It is important that there will be adequate food for all the people that will attend from the surrounding villages.

Chapter 9

As winter continues, the daylight begins to shorten. This requires our trapping and fishing days to start in the dark and return home in the dark. When the mornings are clear and cold, the northern lights are most visible and active. When they are very active, the lights cover the entire sky from horizon to horizon. It is almost magical to run the morning trapline and watch the northern lights dance above our heads. The colder the morning, the more vivid the light show.

According to Pa, the northern lights represent our ancestors dancing in the sky. Pa also believes that these lights are proof that there is a being up in the sky that is responsible for them. No one on earth can create the beauty and motion that we see in the sky. According to Pa, it is more proof of the existence of a supreme being responsible for them.

As the winter snow conditions change, the trail hardens. The sunshine, even with very cold temperatures, causes the snow to melt, then freeze during the night. We need to keep the dogs' feet covered with booties to protect them as the trail becomes harder with more ice forming. Anytime we venture off the trail, we need our snowshoes. The snow will crust over, and every time we fall through the crust, the fluffy snow below makes us go up to our knees. Walking without snowshoes is very hard and physically demanding. The snowshoes help us stay on top of the snow, but we still try to stay on the trail to keep from breaking through.

Traveling on the river becomes increasingly difficult as the river current and ice create pressure ridges. These ridges can grow to several feet tall and create a danger if you run into one of them, but during the night they can be difficult to see. In the day, the ridges cast shadows so they can be seen. Otherwise, it is a white featureless landscape that blends together. Hitting a pressure ridge will almost always break your sled and quickly end your journey.

Every time a person goes out during the day, it is important to watch the sun and not get caught in a sudden storm. Traveling in the black moonless night is only asking for an accident. We avoid going out in the dark when at all possible.

One morning, well after sunrise, we hear the dogs barking outside. We know someone is approaching our cabin. The dogs are telling us that we have a visitor from outside the village. As we open our cabin door, we are greeted by a very cold-looking man with his beard and eyebrows all frosted in white. We invite him in and give him a cup of coffee to warm up. His hands appear as cold as he looks. He wraps them around the hot coffee cup to warm them. Once he warms and is able to remove his parka, fur hat, and mukluks, he begins to explain the purpose of his visit.

He asks for Tungay, who is sitting in the corner working on a trap that is not working correctly. Tungay realizes the person needs his attention and walks toward him. The person explains that his father has suffered an accident near his store. Tungay replies, "Oh no, what happened to my Pa?" The visitor excuses himself and tells Tungay that his name is Ulilek from Mamimuit. "I live next door to Tagneq's store and last night while Tagneq was carrying goods up to his store, he slipped on some ice and fell. According to the doctor, he sprained his ankle, but worse, broke his hip. The doctor has given him medicine to ease the pain and wrapped his hip in a splint and bandaged it," Ulilek explains. Tagneq's wife, Nuliaq, says she needs you to return to Mamimuit as soon as possible to assist with the store's duties.

Tungay, without hesitation, puts the trap that he is holding on the table and begins to gather his clothing and other personal belongings and put them in his personal bag. Arnack gathers some dried fish along with a fresh batch of akutaq and gives them to Ulilek as a meal for the trip back to Mamimuit. Anngaq has already begun hitching Tungay's dogs up to the sled. He empties more personal items that belong to Tungay from the shed and places them in the sled. He covers them with a tarp and ties it to the sled.

While Tungay is putting on his parka, fur hat, and mukluks, he quietly states, "I am so sorry that I have to leave with such short notice. There is so much more winter work to do." "No problem, we will manage," says Pa. Nayagaq tells Tungay, "I will miss you very much, and thank you for the barrette you gave me." Pa opens the cabin door and Tungay's dog team is waiting in the dog yard. As Tungay mounts his sled, I tell him goodbye and wish his Pa a quick recovery.

And just like that, Tungay is gone. We all wave him goodbye, and he turns around and waves back to us as he drops down the riverbank and disappears. Ulilek with his dog team follows behind. We follow Pa into the cabin and discuss our trapline strategy now that Tungay is gone.

Pa tells me, "Qataruaq, you will need to take over Tungay's trapline. Do you think you are able to locate all his snares and traps?" Pa asks. "I think I can find his snares and traps by looking for his foot path as he stopped his sled and walked to each," I say. Pa thinks for a moment and replies, "You are probably right. It hasn't snowed too much since our last trapline run and his snowshoe prints should still be easy to find." I have run Pa's trapline by myself, but Tungay's will be a new experience. I will find out tomorrow.

Tomorrow brings cloudy skies with a little warmer temperature. Since we only have ten dogs, only one sled can be used at a time. Pa helps hitch up the dogs. Just before I take off, Pa asks if I feel confident to run it by myself. I reply with confidence that I will be fine. I make one final equipment check to make sure I have all the survival gear I might need. With a wave to Pa, I untie the rope holding the sled to the smokehouse and off I go.

I follow the west trail to the Kapkaanaq slough cutoff. The alternate trapline that Tungay used is not far up to the place where I go to make the turnoff. I need to pay close attention to the points on the trail where I see his snowshoe tracks that lead to either a snare or trap. I see the first one and stop the sled. I put on the snowshoes and take the club out of the sled and proceed to the site. It is a rabbit snare, but no rabbit today. I only need to sprinkle a little fresh snow around the snare and the rabbit trail to cover my tracks. The next several snares caught a rabbit. They are already frozen, so I do not need the club to kill them. I make any necessary adjustments to the snare and the surrounding snow cover.

The next stop is a trap, and it caught a fox. It is also frozen, so all I have to do is remove it from the trap, reposition the trap, and cover it with new snow. The next several stops are traps with a couple of foxes and one lynx. One trap has a fresh fox, so I have to use my club to kill it first before removing it from the trap. Trapping fox and lynx is not as dangerous as trapping a wolf. When a trap captures a wolf, it is usually still alive and will need to be clubbed to death. Wolves will be very angry when caught in the trap and will lunge at a person, showing their teeth and straining the chain attached to the trap and tree. It is always a very tense situation when approached. You hope the chain attached to the tree holds. The wolf is always jumping, growling, and moving every direction, making a direct head blow with the club difficult. I do not find any wolves in the traps today.

It is a good trapline run today with many rabbits and some foxes and a lynx. As I come to the end of the trapline, it is beginning to get twilight. I need to get back home before it gets dark. As I enter the Kagemuit slough, it is getting dark. The days are so short this time of year. The clouds have gone away and the moonlight on the trail gives me and the dogs a good look at the trail home. As I near Kagemuit, the northern lights are overhead. They are so beautiful to watch them streak and move across the sky. They make concentrating on the trail before me difficult. Thankfully the dogs only focus on the trail and have no concern for the beautiful spectacle above them.

Pa and Anngaq meet me in the dog yard. Pa unhitches the dogs and Anngaq is preparing the dog soup. I notice in the distance near the shed some new dogs are tied up where Tungay had his dog yard. I ask Pa, "Where did these dogs come from?" He says, "I will tell you during our evening meal," as we both open the door of the cabin to the smell of moose roast on the cookstove.

During our evening meal, Pa explains how he went to his brothers Kevig and Arlunaq to explain the situation about how Tungay had to leave suddenly and now he had only one dog team to use for running his two traplines. They had extra dogs, so they let me have them for the rest of the winter. Qavcik also gave me two of her dogs to help our situation. Now we have sixteen dogs to make two teams of eight dogs each. Pa explains that with two fewer dogs per team, we may have to shorten our traplines so we don't overwork each team. Now with two dog sleds we can keep the four traplines. Without a second team, we would have to eliminate the traplines that Tungay was using.

As the winter progresses, I become good friends with Robert, the teacher from northern Idaho. He knows I am a very good outdoorsman as I follow my Pa's native ways. He talks with me often about fishing, hunting, and trapping as he lived in a country home outside a small town. He has never heard about net fishing under the ice in a river. He went ice fishing on frozen lakes with a short fishing rod. He cut the holes in the ice with an auger that he turned with a handle at the top. I think that sounds so much easier and faster than using an ice pick. He also has a trapline near his house that he runs during the winter. His stories about hunting big animals like moose, elk, and bear really fascinate me.

Over time we become very close friends as I take him on my trapline journeys. He is most impressed with our tundra that is new to him. He lives in the mountains and is more familiar with living among the trees. He tells me about the hound dogs that he keeps for bobcat hunting. These wild cats are like our lynx but climb trees when the hounds try to catch them.

He is very impressed with our skill at net fishing under the river ice. He is a great addition to our ability to cut holes in the ice with our ice picks. He is very muscular with his endurance to simply keep the ice pick going forever. Pa is very impressed with his strength. Pa says, "Robert can really go with that ice pick." Pa is very impressed with Robert even though he is a white man. Pa would not admit it, but I think he really likes him when he comes along to help us. Robert wants to learn about our native ways. Pa is going to teach him everything he needs to know about our Eskimo ways. Robert helps us with getting water from the river. He is able to carry two buckets with ease from the river. His wood cutting and splitting skills are another great help for us. He always makes certain we are full of split wood ready for our cookstove. He not only helps us but makes every effort to help grandpa with his wood supply. He has plenty of experience with wood cutting as he heats his house with wood back in Idaho.

Ma makes certain he is well fed each time he comes over to help us. Eventually he acquires an appetite for our dried fish and akutaq dessert.

Nayagaq makes bread more often as Robert looks forward to eating her fresh bread. Everyone in my family enjoys his humor and jokes that he shares with us during his visits.

One afternoon while my entire family is cutting fish that we caught from our river net fishing, Kenruk comes by to talk with us. Kenruk is my cousin and is my best friend in the whole village. We spend a lot of time together when we are not working with our families. Kenruk walks over to Pa and asks, "I want to live with you." Pa looks over to Ma while she is cutting fish, and she with an approving nod of her head and a smile on her face agrees. Kenruk takes his place in the fish processing and helps to carry the fish to the smokehouse. The fish that are not smoked are taken inside the cabin to become part of the evening meal.

I am very happy to have Kenruk live with us. Now that he is a part of our family, I don't need to go over to his cabin to get him. After we complete the fish cutting, Kenruk and I go behind our cabin and continue our work on the igloo that we were building a few days before. I tell Kenruk that I am very happy to have him living with us. We only get a couple of snow blocks added to our igloo when Nayagaq calls for us to come for the evening meal. It is going to be a wonderful meal with Kenruk now a part of our family.

We know Christmas is coming when the teachers bring an evergreen tree to the school building and decorate it with ornaments that are stored in the school supply room. Anngaq is in his last year of school. Kuvak is in the third grade and Algaq is in her first year of school. Kuvak and Algaq are excited with the prospect of being a part of the school's Christmas program. Eskimos do not celebrate Christmas in our cabin as it is just another day in our subsistence life. We have no access to an evergreen tree and ornaments to bring into our cabin. To our way of thinking, it is just a white man's holiday.

Christmas also comes during the shortest days of the year. We don't get complete darkness, but the short duration of daylight allows us to be outside for only a short time before night falls. The northern lights are at their peak this time of year.

Anngaq brings a note home from school announcing the Christmas program will be held tomorrow evening, which is Christmas Eve. The school will provide an evening meal. It is what white people call American holiday food. On our way to the Christmas program, we stop to bring grandpa and grandma along with us to the school building. They have not been to the school building since the flood evacuation.

Everyone in the village is present in the school building to be a part of the Christmas program. The meal consists of roast turkey, dressing, potatoes, carrots, and cranberry sauce. The cranberry sauce came from a can. For dessert we have pumpkin pie and ice cream. This is the only time of year when we eat these foods. After the meal, the school-age children present the nativity pageant that represents the birth of Jesus Christ. I am a little confused about the meaning of the play. Shamanism and Eskimo creation stories do not mention this person as an important figure in history from a very far away land. During the nativity play the children sing religious songs about the birth of Jesus.

After the play we wait for the entry of Santa Claus. I am not sure what this person has to do with religion, but his appearance always excites the young children. He brings a large sack that holds a gift and a small box of candy that he gives to each child. Even the children too young to be in school receive a gift and a small box of candy. I recognize that Santa Claus is my teacher friend Robert. He makes the children very happy and excited with his presence.

After the gifts and candy are distributed, everyone leaves the building and goes home. As we walk home, we are entertained by ancient relatives dancing in the sky as our northern lights display. It is a very cold walk back to our cabin. Our breath from everyone creates a frosty cloud ahead of us. During our time at school, Robert asks if he and I could go hunting tomorrow morning. I agree as he insists it is his only time that he will be available to hunt as there is no school on Christmas day.

The morning begins with warmer temperatures as some clouds formed during the night. As the sun rises, Robert knocks on the cabin door. We welcome him with a cup of coffee that he accepts. Pa explains that the weather feels strange. He suggests we should reconsider our hunt and delay it to another day. Robert states that this is his only opportunity to go hunting during a day off for Christmas. Pa, with hesitation in his voice, states, "Well, if you have to go, keep a watch for an incoming storm. I don't feel good because the weather could worsen at any time," Pa explains in his fatherly tone. He emphasizes that we make certain to bring our emergency supplies if we need to use them.

Anngaq has the dogs ready to go as Robert and I leave the cabin. I drive and Robert sits in the sled basket. We take the west route and follow the Kagemuit slough to the place where it goes south and deeper into the tundra. Willows along the slough are a good environment for ptarmigans to nest and find safety from the tundra winds. This is also good cover for finding rabbits.

We stop the sled and put on our snowshoes to venture among the willows. Ptarmigan can be difficult to spot except for their black eye, which is what we look for among the white tundra background. Robert spots a ptarmigan at the base of a willow tree finding shelter from the cold wind. He takes aim and makes an accurate kill. Robert proves to be a very good shot, just like Tungay. He picks up the bird and we continue hunting the willows.

It is a good day for ptarmigan hunting. Robert states he would really like to kill a rabbit. The tundra rabbits turn white in the winter, thus making them difficult to spot just like the white ptarmigan. We decide that better rabbit hunting is further down the slough. We get back on the sled and continue our journey. As Pa said, the weather begins to change. Robert is determined to get a rabbit, so we continue, although I am not sure it is a good idea. We approach another area that looks promising for rabbit, so we stop the sled and walk into the willow patch. We see rabbit signs that give us some optimism, but no rabbits. The weather continues to close in on us as we continue walking the willows. Just as I am about to tell Robert we should end the hunt and start for home, he says, "I see one just near the big willow to my left." We both stop and Robert takes aim with his rifle. He shoots and kills the rabbit with a good head shot. He hurries to pick up the rabbit and we quickly retreat to the sled. The dogs seem nervous as they sense a storm is coming.

We turn the sled around and head back to Kagemuit. The dogs obey my turnaround command as they are ready to go home. The snow starts to fall and quickly begins to fall heavily. I tell myself we can handle the snowfall if the wind does not pick up. It is beginning to get twilight, so darkness will soon be upon us. This is when the wind begins to blow much harder and it is hard to see the slough before us. I have to yell to get Robert's attention as the wind is creating a lot of noise around us. I tell Robert, "We are going to have to stop and find shelter along the slough bank."

I stop the sled and search for my snow saw that I packed away in my emergency bag. I explain to Robert that we will need to build some shelter using the bank of the slough and make a fort to give us shelter. As I proceed to cut snow blocks with my saw, I tell Robert to look for some willow branches and wood to make a fire once we get the shelter enclosed. It is really snowing heavily, and the wind hurts my exposed skin. Making an igloo as a kid for fun now takes on a survival level of need. Thankfully the slough bank makes the work go faster as I only need three sides and a roof. Since the wind is coming from the southwest, I can leave the front of the shelter mostly open unless the wind changes direction.

Robert has gathered enough wood, so he is able to help me position the snow blocks for the roof. This is the tricky part of the build—to shape the blocks so they fit together as an arch shape over the top. The wind makes every cut in the deep tundra snow difficult as the cold begins to hurt my face. I hope I am not getting frostbite. We position the last snow block on the roof. Our emergency igloo is now complete and ready to occupy. Our attention shifts to the dogs, but they really don't need any help as they find shelter and comfort against the bank of the slough. They are already covered with insulating snow and seem very content with the situation.

I turn the sled on its side and bring the emergency bag inside the igloo. Robert and I work together to get a fire going so we can melt the snow blocks to seal the inside of the igloo. I fill a pot with snow and place it in the fire to melt hot water to make coffee. Inside the bag are dried fish and bread from Nayagaq. While the blizzard rages outside, we are comfortable in our emergency igloo. Robert comments, "I will probably not make it back in time to start school tomorrow." I try to assure him that I think the weather may break during the night.

While we sit around the fire, I tell Robert about my first rabbit catch. We are not far from where I caught my first rabbit. I could not keep it as our tradition requires us to give our first catch to an older person. I gave my rabbit to grandpa. By doing so, we are granted a successful hunting life and show respect to our elders. "That is a wonderful tradition that even white people should live by," Robert says. "Too many of our possessions are not shared with those in need, especially with respect for those older than us," remarks Robert. We are both very tired, so we soon go to sleep. Rather than putting the fire out, we keep it going during the night.

Morning breaks just as I predicted. The snow has stopped, and the wind is no longer blowing. Robert is in a hurry to get back to the school building, so we pack the emergency bag and crawl out of the igloo. It is still dark, but the moon lights the trail. The dogs are completely covered in snow but loving every moment as they know we will be on our way back home. With a brilliant northern light display above, we make our way back to Kagemuit.

As Robert exits the sled, he comments, "I think I will get school started right on time after all." He gathers his ptarmigans and rabbit and hurries toward the school building. I enter the cabin and Ma responds, "So, you finally made it home. Do you want a morning meal?" "Yes, I am starving!" I reply. "You got caught in the weather that I warned you about," says Pa in an "I told you so" attitude. "Yes, you were correct," I say in a tone of humility. "I never worried about you because you learned all the survival ways that I taught you," Pa states just like a good teacher. "I did as you taught me, Pa," is my reply. Before I get the words out of my mouth, Ma shoves a plate of pancakes in front of me and a hot cup of coffee. Nayagaq gives me a hug that only a sister can give. "I worried about you all night," she says with tears forming in her eyes. Kenruk adds, "All those play igloos that we built finally paid off."

"In a few days a new year will be upon us," says Pa. We sit quietly and wonder among ourselves in our small cabin what the new year will bring us.

Chapter 10

Kenruk and I have taken over Tungay's trapline. Both the west and north traplines are good producers. Many rabbits are caught. The rabbit population is showing that it is on the rise of its cycle this winter. Our trapping for fox and lynx has been very good. We have caught a few wolves, but not many.

Kenruk had been taught the native ways by his father Kevig. He is a great help not only running the trapline, but his fishing skills help with the fish traps and river net fishing. With the upcoming potlatch, the entire village is engaged to provide extra fish to feed the visitors. The black fish we trap in the slough are placed in the cold storage pit. It is a good year for catching black fish, and every family is reporting an abundance of them.

River netting under the ice has been good, but not great. With Kenruk helping with ice chipping as we set our nets under the ice, we can go out more often and try to increase our catch. The extra whitefish, sheefish, and pike we catch are cut and hung in the smokehouse to store them for potlatch food. The burbot are eaten during our meals as they don't store well for any extended time.

Just as the men of the village are busy with outdoor work, the women are busy making gifts for those attending the potlatch. Grass weaving is the work of every woman in the village. Many grass baskets and grass dolls are being made to be given away. Ma is making moose skin YoYos as gifts. Since Nayagaq and Anngaq are having their first dance this potlatch, she is extra busy making gifts to be given during their first dance.

When a young person is having their first dance, a new kuspuk and headdress is made for the girl. A new shirt is made for the boy to celebrate this special event in his life. Pa makes a new grass handle, and Ma attaches large feathers to the one that Anngaq will use. Nayagaq's dance fan is made with a grass handle and decorated with bead work and short feathers. The girl's dance fan is much more ornate to represent the beauty of the Yupik woman.

In preparation for Nayagaq's dance, she has chosen "fish cutting" as her dance theme. Anngaq has chosen "running the dog sled" as his dance theme. They spend a lot of time practicing their dance motions. Both Pa and Ma assist them in perfecting their dance routines. My parents discuss the dance themes with grandpa as he is the elder drummer, and he is the lead drummer for the village. It is important for the lead drummer to understand the dance theme to coordinate the drum beat and song that will be used. Grandpa agrees that their dance theme is appropriate, and he approves their choice.

With grandpa approving their dance theme, they begin their practice to memorize each motion during the dance. It is a proud moment for not only the first dancer, but also the parents and family when performing in front of the potlatch gathering. A well-performed first dance brings great honor to the entire family. A first dance will be remembered for a person's entire lifetime. It is a rite of passage for each young person to perform their first dance.

It is late afternoon while we are cutting fish from the net fishing catch when Ukurraq, Kenruk's Ma, comes to our cabin. She is very distraught and shaken as she tells us that Kevig is very late returning from his trip to Mamimuit. She is concerned that something has happened to him. Teruluk, her daughter, had come down with an illness. She was taken to Emily, the village nurse, to be examined. Emily indicates that Teruluk requires medicine that she does not have among her medical supplies. She needs an antibiotic that she is not qualified to administer. She advises that a doctor in Mamimuit can give her the medication needed. Kevig left with his dog team to go to Mamimuit and bring the medicine back to Teruluk. "He is long overdue, and I fear something has happened to him," states Ukurraq in a worried voice. "How do you know that?" asks Pa. She tells him that his dog team returned to her cabin without Kevig. The tow rope was still attached to a part of his sled as though it had broken due to a possible accident. It certainly appears that Kevig is stranded somewhere on the river below Kagemuit. "We have to go quickly and look for Pa," says Kenruk with a very concerned look on his face. His father needs help somewhere on the river and it is already dark outside.

Kenruk runs to his cabin to bring back Kevig's runaway dog team so he can hitch them to Anngaq's sled. When he returns to our cabin, I have Pa's dog team hitched to my sled. I have loaded my sled with my emergency bag, blankets, and a tarp to bring Kevig back in my sled. In quick time both Kenruk and I leave the village and head down to the river. Hopefully Kevig's dogs can lead us to where Kevig is stranded.

It is very black dark out as there is a cloudy sky and a new moon which provides no light to help us see very well. Our only assistance we have to guide us is the pure white snow on the river and willows on the side of the bank which give us a landmark to keep us on the river. We must go slow in order to see ahead enough to avoid hitting a pressure ridge. The slower we go, the longer it will take us to find Kevig. Not a hopeful situation that we are confronting. Kenruk takes the lead, and I follow close behind.

I wonder in my mind how far downriver we must journey until we find Kevig. Many possibilities go through my mind. How will we find him from a health standpoint? I have no experience with aiding medical emergencies. A broken sled I can mend. A broken body is another problem I am not sure I can mend. It is so dark to see anything. The pressure ridges come up so quickly when it is this dark. Open water is a very real hazard. The ice can open because of river currents and pressure ridges that lead to a separation of the river ice. Falling into open water can lead to a life-threatening situation quickly. I try not to think about that situation. I try to focus on driving my sled and not on the possible worst-case scenarios.

I pull my sled up to Kenruk and try to ease my anxiety by asking him what he thinks could have happened to his Pa. The despair in his face is the only answer I get. "Does he always carry an emergency bag?" I ask. A simple, yes, is his reply. The snow on the river ice is deep enough to keep ourselves quiet. If Kevig tries to get our attention with his voice, we should be able to hear him.

More pressure ridges develop as we enter a narrow section of the river. I sure hope we don't hit one of these because we can't see them. Pa's dogs which I chose to use because they are experienced enough to avoid dangerous ice. I place my confidence in them to keep me safe. The wind begins to pick up, which only makes our situation more difficult. The wind makes it harder to listen to our surroundings.

In the distance Kenruk yells to me, "I think I see something that looks like a fire on the riverbank to the right." "Yes, I do see that," I respond. As we come closer, we can identify a fire burning for sure. There is a person sitting next to the fire as we approach. Kenruk calls from his sled, "Pa, is that you!" "Yes, it is me, Kenruk," says the shadow of a person behind the fire.

We now rush our sleds toward the fire and Kevig is sitting next to it. As we approach, I can see that he is hurt and not moving very easily. He also looks very cold and is shivering due to the windy conditions. Kenruk asks, "Are you hurt?" Kevig replies, "I have bruises all over my body." He does not think any bones are broken. I mention to Kevig that I don't see his sled anywhere. He says with a little fun in his voice, "What is left of it is in the fire." "What happened?" both Kenruk and I ask in unison. He explains that it was very dark, and the wind was blowing the snow so that I could not see the pressure ridge ahead of me. The dogs quickly maneuvered around it, but my sled did not. I hit it at full speed. The sled broke into many pieces and the dogs kept on going. Kenruk remarks that the dogs came back to the cabin with the front end of your sled still attached to the tow rope.

"Are you able to walk to my sled?" I ask him. "Only with your help," he replies. Kenruk and I help him to my sled and place him in the sled basket. I cover him with the blankets that I brought. I put a tarp over him to keep him protected from the wind. "I will try to drive smoothly, but I am not sure if I can promise a smooth ride home," I tell him. "I will be happy to just get back to my cabin," Kevig says.

As we pull up to Kevig's cabin, we are greeted by his wife, Ukurraq, and his three children. It is a wonderful reunion as Ukurraq gives him a kiss, while Teruluk, Nayak, and Cetaaq give him a hug. Kenruk and I help Kevig into the cabin and set him on the bed. We will have Emily come over tomorrow and examine you when she is available.

Kevig opens a pocket of his parka and removes a bottle with a piece of paper. He hands it to Ukurraq. "This is the medicine with instructions that Teruluk needs to take for her sickness," Kevig says. "I am so sorry you had to get hurt because of me," Teruluk says with tears in her eyes and a huge hug to her Pa. "You would sacrifice all you have for your family," Ukurraq says with another loving kiss to Kevig. "What about your sled?" asks Cetaaq. "I had to use it to make a signal fire since it was very broken from hitting the pressure ridge," Kevig says. "You can use Pa's old sled while he builds you a new one," I say. He remarks that would be very generous of him.

Kenruk and I bring our dog teams back to my cabin. Kenruk unhitches Kevig's dogs and brings them back to their own dog yard. Once I am in my cabin, everyone wants to hear what happened. I give them a complete recap of our journey. It is very late when Kenruk returns to the cabin and we both enjoy a warm meal of fish soup and tea. Tomorrow will be another day.

The next day in the afternoon, we bring Pa's old sled over to Kevig's cabin. Emily is leaving their cabin as we approach. We ask her about Kevig's condition. She says he has a lot of bruises and since he hit his head during the accident, he has had a bad headache that may last a few days. Kenruk and I enter the cabin to see Kevig take some of the medicine that Emily gave him. "This is to help relieve the pain according to Emily," he says. "I sure hope it works because I feel bruised everywhere on my body," Kevig grimaces as he speaks. "How are you feeling, Teruluk?" Kenruk asks. "I do feel a bit better," she says. "Qataruaq and I brought over Unozroak's old sled for you to use once you get healed," Kenruk says. "That means a lot to me. You are very helpful. Give my thanks to your Pa," Kevig says with satisfaction in his voice. "He is more than happy to help you," I reply.

The winter continues as the snow depth gets deeper and the river ice thickens. Everyone in the village gets into a routine of subsistence living. The time of potlatch gets closer while we try to make preparations and stock up on our food supplies in anticipation of a good turnout from the nearby villages.

We make any repairs to the communal house or qasgiq as we call it in our Yupik language. Since it is the pride of every village, there is always someone keeping it in good condition. It is the center of the universe we call our village. We use it often whenever the village has an activity. The qasgiq is located next to the slough between the cabins of Kevig and Arlunaq. It is the largest and most prominent building in the village.

It has a round shape on the outside walls. It is built so there are no corners on the inside of the structure. The outside is covered with mud from the base where it meets the ground to the dome-shaped roof. The roof is also covered in mud. There is a hole in the top of the roof to let the smoke escape while being used as a sauna or fire house. There is one main entrance to the building. There is a fire pit in the center that is used to provide light when used while it is dark outside.

As the day of the potlatch approaches, everyone makes last-minute preparations. The drummers and dancers practice often to make certain every participant is well practiced. The drummers check their drums to make sure they are tight and sound correct. Nayagaq and Anngaq practice their first dance every day. They want to show the people the pride of their family.

The day of the potlatch arrives. We expect to see Ma's brothers and sister arrive from Kwigamuit. Cakiraq's brothers and sisters are coming from Kameglimiut. There may be a few families who arrive from Mamimuit. I don't think Tungay or his parents will come as Tagneq is still recovering from his hip injury.

Shortly after noon, Arnack's oldest brother Taruq and his wife Hungaq along with their two children arrive for the potlatch. The four of them will stay with us. Our cabin will be quite full with them staying with us. I am happy they chose to stay with us. I remember Taruq giving Ma one of his wolf pelts. She proudly shows him the garment she sewed using it. Hungaq is envious of the excellent quality of the garment that Ma made. Hungaq responds as she examines it, "This is so beautiful, and the beadwork is the finest I have ever seen." From one of the bags Hungaq brought, she takes out a crock that contains sourdough starter and hands it to Ma. Ma is very happy as she thanks Hungaq. "I have always wanted to make a sourdough starter but never got around to it," Ma says with her excited voice. From the same bag, Taruq hands Pa a new leghold trap to add to his trapping supplies. Pa is very happy and tells Taruq, "This is a very needed trap as some of mine are getting old and need to be replaced."

"I do have sad news to tell you, Arnack. Ma and Pa died during early fall," Taruq directs his words at Arnack. Ma drops her head and says, "That does not surprise me as I knew they were having difficulties when we visited before fish camp." Taruq explains that they both caught a late summer cold and could not recover. I took them to the doctor in Mamimuit. He provided them with medicine, but it did not help them improve. We buried them in the cemetery behind the village. Ma takes the news better than I expected. She does not mourn for long as she becomes her joyful self again and is happy that everyone could visit the potlatch. Ma knows that life happens, and we must go ahead and move forward.

Taruq tells us that his sister and her family are planning to stay with grandpa and grandma. Ma says with an agreeing smile, "I am sure they will be more than happy to host your sister's family." They should be there now as they were right behind us with their dog team as we entered Kagemuit. Taruq explains that his younger brother and his family were going to stay with Arlunaq and Kiak.

We explain that the school will allow any visitors to stay in their building. "That is what we were planning as my youngest brother is planning to stay at the school," Taruq says. Since he has the largest family with his wife and four children, his large family might overwhelm a family cabin. "There will be plenty of room for them at the school building," Pa explains. "I think I hear your dogs becoming restless and barking outside," Anngaq says from his corner of the cabin. Pa, Anngaq, Taruq, and I go outside to untie the dogs from the sled and tie them to the shed behind the smokehouse. Anngaq brings a bunch of grass to bed the dogs on the snow. They immediately lay on the fresh, dry grass and go to sleep. I am sure they are very tired from the trip from Kwigamuit.

Pa asks if it has been a good trapping season. Taruq replies, "Not as good as last year. It has been a fantastic rabbit catch, but the traps have not produced like they did last year." Pa tells Taruq that our rabbit catch has been excellent also this year. Pa tells the story of our trail mishap while hitting a fallen tree on the trapline. "I had just built that sled this season and then I had to repair it," Pa says with a humble grin. Taruq adds, "You never know what can happen on the trapping trail."

Ma thinks we should go over and make sure her sister is getting settled at grandpa's cabin. Everyone follows Ma as she leads us to grandpa's cabin. Her sister's dog team is laying in the snow in front of the cabin. We wake them as we approach. Ma gives her sister a big hug and greets her husband and child.

Ma hasn't seen her sister for a long time as she was not in Kwigamuit when we stopped during the spring resupply trip to Mamimuit. The two are very happy to see each other. Grandma is very happy to have them stay at their cabin during the potlatch.

Grandpa offers coffee and tea to everyone, so we are required to stay longer than we had expected. We have a great time visiting. Grandpa shows everyone a nice pair of mittens that Ma's sister made for him as a gift. Grandma is given a beautiful hair barrette with fancy beadwork that she shows with pride. "I will show this to everyone at the potlatch tonight," she says with that grandma smile of hers. We finish our hot drinks and tell grandpa that we will tend to the dogs and get them bedded down for the night. "Anngaq will take good care of the dogs," Grandpa assures everyone.

Ma tells me and Kenruk to go to Arlunaq's cabin and the school to make certain the rest of her two brothers' families are settled in for the potlatch weekend. Both families are comfortable at Arlunaq's family and at the school building. The children are certainly having fun in the wide-open school building. We return to confirm that her brothers arrived and are being well cared for.

When Kenruk and I enter our cabin, everyone is waiting for us with the evening meal already prepared and ready to eat. It is a wonderful feeling to hear everyone having a good time visiting while we enjoy the delicious meal that Ma has prepared.

As soon as we finish the evening meal and the dishes are washed, we ready ourselves to depart to the communal house for the evening portion of the potlatch. On our way we stop to have everyone at grandpa's cabin join us as we walk together. We stop at Kevig's cabin to find out that Cakiraq's sister has not arrived from Kameglimiut. He says Cakiraq's brothers and sisters will not arrive until tomorrow.

We arrive at the qasgiq, and our group is the only one that has entered so far. It is still twilight as Pa starts the fire in the fire pit to provide some light and heat. Grandma complains that it is cold inside and she is not going to take her parka off until it warms up. Pa assures her it will warm up quickly with the fire and all the bodies gathered inside. Pa goes to each lamp and lights them for additional illumination. With the fire going and all the lamps lit, the qasgiq begins to warm and is well lit. Just as it becomes comfortable inside, Ma's youngest brother and his family arrive. She gives her brother a big hug and a kiss to his wife. The four children wait for their turn to receive their hug from Ma. They are so happy to see her again.

A little later two families from Mamimuit enter the qasgiq. One family we recognize from a previous potlatch that we attended. The other family we have not seen before. We welcome them both and exchange greetings with everyone. Now that we are all together and seated, Pa walks to the center near the fire pit to offer a welcome to those in attendance. With the fire crackling and illuminating his face, Pa gives his welcome words.

"I want to welcome everyone to our potlatch. All the people of Kagemuit welcome you. We want this celebration of our Yupik life to be a challenge to your life. I hope that as you leave our village you will be encouraged by our presence, our love, our drummers and dancers, and most of all our wise words lead your life. We want you to enjoy your time here and embrace each other's welcoming joy. The land has provided us with a bounty of fish and fruit that we want to share with you during your stay. The women have been busy making gifts to share with each of you. Every food and gift are brought to you from our deepest heart and gratitude. I now invite you to welcome our wise words speaker for tonight, Apak, our most respected elder."

Apak walks to the edge of the fire pit and introduces himself to the gathering. "I am Apak, originally from a now abandoned village downriver from Kagemuit. Emak and I settled here because we thought it provided us with a new beginning. This land has been good to us. When you respect the land, it will provide an abundance to your existence.

"Every family begins with children. They are the fruit of our life as mother and father. I want to invite all the young children to come and sit by the fire pit as I want to talk to you." The young children come forward and sit around the fire pit. "You are the future of our people. You are dependent upon your parents for your very survival and existence. As you grow and mature into young adults, I want you to always remember and follow the wise words spoken to you by your parents. The wise words are seeds planted in your life to grow and make you a worthy member of your village.

"Remember to always honor your parents. Do as they say. You show them respect and honor by obeying them. As you grow, do not dishonor your parents by not allowing the wise word seeds to flourish inside of you.

When your parents tell you to do something, do it without hesitation. It honors them and they will love you for it. When your life shows that your wise word seeds are bearing good fruit, you give everyone in your village a good feeling for a bountiful harvest.

"As I am sending you back to your family, I am grateful for your attention. Keep wise words always in your life and especially in your heart.

"Now I want to talk to the young adults. Wise words are important to you. You have heard the wise words, and it is up to you to use them. The wise words that have been spoken to you should make you desire to use them to show respect to those who spoke them and everyone in the village that watches you use them. You are an important member of the family unit. Bring honor to your family. Remember that a relationship between a boy and girl is to honor each other. That honor bears itself by not having sexual relationships. You must wait until you get married. That is the Yupik way.

"To you young men, learn the Eskimo life by watching your father and learning the subsistence life they are passing down to you as a son. You must learn these lifestyles so you can support a family when you are the father. You honor your father by using his teachings and applying them to your everyday life.

"To you young women, also pay attention to your mother and learn her ways. You are a great help to the family when you can do the work as a mother. Your mother will be given honor when you show her that you are willing to assist and perform her duties when she requests them.

"Lastly, you young adults should desire to show the village that you are willing to take the mantle of wise words into our next generation. A village with strong young adults is a village destined to become everlasting and lead the village when your turn begins.

"Now I will talk to your parents. As a little person is one that listens to wise words, and a young adult is one that uses wise words, you are the speakers of wise words. You are responsible for shaping your children in the ways of the Yupik. You do this by talking to them using wise words. You cannot rely upon only your elders to do all this work. Your children look up to you as their elder to teach them the right way of living. They will listen to your words, but it is your life that they see you live to back up your words. Words alone will not convince them; it is your actions that they will see and follow.

"Fathers: you are the leader of the family. You are the provider. It is you that your family relies upon to provide food, skins, and leadership. You need to be strong and give an example of one that speaks wise words.

"Mothers: you are the glue that binds the family. Love your husband and honor him. Love your children and show them you care about their welfare. You are a helpmate to your husband. It takes both a mother and father to provide the family structure that makes a village great.

"Always carry a walking stick with you. This walking stick or ayaruq will lead you in the right way. It is the wise words that help you decide which path to take. Whether it be a newly frozen river or snow-covered tundra, it will help you lead the way. When it is properly used, it will keep you safe and walking the right path. When a decision is required, it helps you make the right choice.

"As elders, we are the leaders of our village. Our residents rely on us to make good choices for them when we are asked. This requires us to consider our words and actions. Everyone listens to us and watches our actions. This is an important responsibility that we take seriously. When we fail to give wise words, we have failed our village.

"This is all I have to say. I give my fire back to Unozroak to give any final words before we leave for the night." Apak walks to Emak and sits next to her. Unozroak steps forward and thanks everyone for attending and hopes the wise words spoken we carry in our hearts. He tells everyone to come back tomorrow evening for a time to share with drumming and dancing.

Everyone leaves the qasgiq and returns to their own cabins. It is very dark outside with clear skies and it is very cold. Above us the northern lights are very active and cover the sky from horizon to horizon. It is as though our ancient ancestors are telling us that we have heard powerful wise words, and they are proud of them and the one who spoke them.

As we enter our cabin, Pa stokes the cookstove fire and heats the water pot for coffee and tea. As we enjoy our beverage, we discuss the wise words that we just heard. We conclude our evening with everyone in the cabin finding a place to bed. As I go to sleep, I am happy for this day and look forward to tomorrow.

I wake up to a warm cabin and smell of fresh boiled coffee as Pa woke up early to restart the fire. Ma is busy using her new sourdough starter to make pancakes for our morning meal. Hungaq is showing Ma how to add flour, sugar, and salt to the starter to make pancakes. We all have a good meal to start our second day of potlatch.

When the sun finally rises, Kenruk and I go to every cabin and the school looking for children willing to play outside. We tell them to meet at the communal house. We plan to play ice hockey on the river as a group. We prepare a court on the river ice by clearing the snow with our shovel and broom. Earlier, before the day of the potlatch arrived, we cut a bunch of willows to use as our hockey sticks. A simple ball is used as a puck.

Not all the children desire to play hockey on the ice. Those that want to play a different game can do so. Some want to build an igloo, so we assist in the construction of one in front of the qasgiq. The smallest children are content to play hide and seek in the school building. The parents are kept busy watching their own children play in the game of their choice.

The days are getting longer, but twilight comes quickly, and the evening meal is being prepared by each family. As Kenruk and I enter our cabin, both Anngaq and Nayagaq are practicing their individual first dance. They seem ready for their chance to dance before the people at the potlatch.

During the afternoon, Cakiraq's brothers and sisters arrive from Kameglimiut with their dog teams. Cakiraq's oldest brother and his family are staying with Qavcik and Cakiraq across the slough in their cabin. Cakiraq's oldest sister and her family are staying with Kevig and Ukurraq next to the slough and grandpa's cabin. Cakiraq's youngest sister and her family will stay at the school. The three extra dog teams cause the rest of the dogs in the village to become restless and begin barking. It creates a very noisy village with all the dogs barking.

We complete our evening meal and prepare to leave the cabin for the potlatch. Pa brings his drum and drumstick as he will be one of the drummers along with his brothers to provide the drum beat for the dancers. We all dress up for this special occasion as my entire family will participate in the dances. Even my youngest, Algaq and Kuvak, are dressed to participate in the dancing.

We arrive at the qasgiq to find Kevig and Arlunaq tightening their drum skins and spraying water mist on them to provide the correct sound they desire. Pa prepares his drum and sprays mist on it to give his drum the right sound that he wants.

Cakiraq and Qavcik enter with her family. They are followed by Cakiraq's brothers and his two sisters and their families. Cakiraq gives his drum a spray of water mist. All the drummers are ready, and they take their place on the drummer stage.

Grandpa with his drum takes his place in the middle of the group as the lead drummer. Grandpa announces that the first song is to recognize Nayagaq with her first dance. The title of the dance is "cutting fish." Grandpa begins the drumming, and the other drummers follow with their drums. Kenruk and I follow the village dancers onto the stage and begin the dance. Nayagaq enters the stage in the front and begins the motions with her dance fans of her fish cutting dance. The other dancers behind her follow her motions. We repeat the "fish cutting" dance several times and then the dance ends. Nayagaq performs very well, and when she finishes, the audience applauds their approval of a dance well done. Nayagaq knows she has done well with the smile on her face as her own approval.

Grandpa then announces that Anngaq will be performing his first dance, and it is titled "running the dog sled." Grandpa begins drumming with the others following. Anngaq takes his place in the front row of the dancers. He begins his motions imitating running the dogs, and the other dancers follow his motions in unison. Again, the dance is performed several times and then the dance ends. Anngaq is rewarded with a dance well done to the applause of the audience. He recognizes their appreciation with his raised hand and a shake of his head.

Now that the first dancers have finished, Ma takes the sack that holds the gifts that she has made and gives one to each family present. Everyone is excited and grateful for the gift that Ma gives. After Ma distributes the gifts, she takes her place on the stage with the Kagemuit dancers.

Grandpa announces the next dance that will be "the berry picking dance." All the dancers do very well and provide a wonderful atmosphere of excitement as the dance rises in intensity toward the end. The next dance is called "net fishing." The final dance of the evening is titled "the northern lights." Grandpa gives the audience his version of the lights as a remembrance of our ancestors dancing in the sky. The motions are very vibrant and colorful to reflect the beauty of the northern lights. As the last round of the dance begins, grandpa announces that it is now an "all dance" that allows the entire audience to come to the stage and participate. Almost the entire audience comes forward to share in the dance and fills the stage to capacity. As the dance continues, the drummers increase their beat, and the drums are very loud now. All the dancers move with increasing excitement with everyone having a wonderful time dancing. Eventually the dance comes to its conclusion.

The drummers stop while all the dancers congratulate and encourage each other. It is a moment to remember for a potlatch enjoyed by everyone. Many hugs are shared knowing that all the visitors will depart the following morning to their separate villages. It will be another year until the next potlatch is scheduled to be held in the village of Kameglimiut, Cakiraq's home village.

Just like last night, the air is cold as we depart the qasgiq. We see a breath fog leading our way home in front of us. The ever-present northern lights dance overhead. Before we enter the cabin, Pa asks if everyone is ready for coffee and tea to celebrate our first dancers Nayagaq and Anngaq. We all agree as we step inside the warm cabin.

Nayagaq and Anngaq thank everyone for their first dance performance. They admit that it was a total village accomplishment. They especially acknowledge Ma and Pa for their complete encouragement to overcome their fear of making a mistake during their first dance. They did well as they crossed their line of maturity into the family of village dancers.

I am so excited to be a part of their success that it makes it so difficult to go to sleep. It is a great day for our village and especially my family, which I am very proud of. I eventually find my rest and go to sleep.

I think everyone must have been very tired as no one wakes up early. It is almost sunrise before any of us get up from our sleep. As usual, it is Pa that wakes up first and restarts the fire and has the water ready to boil for coffee and tea. Ma prepares our morning meal knowing that Taruq, Hungaq, and their two children will be leaving to travel back to Kwigamuit.

They want to get an early start to their journey, so Anngaq, Kenruk, and I hitch Taruq's dogs to his sled and have it ready for them at our cabin's front door. In a short time, Ma's other sister's dog team arrives at our cabin. Trailing right behind are her two younger brothers' dog teams. Ma gives each of them a hug and a kiss before they prepare to leave. All their children wait their turn to give Ma a long hug before each walks back to their sled and settles in for the ride back to Kwigamuit.

It is a noisy goodbye as all the dogs are barking and jumping, more than ready to get on the trail. As the four dog teams leave for the river, there is not a dry eye among my family as we run to the riverbank to give our final waves to the sleds disappearing in the distance. Ma says with tears in her eyes, "I already miss them so much. There is never enough time to share our lives with the ones so precious to us." Pa gives Ma a loving hug to provide what comfort he can offer.

We go back to our cabin and wait for the evening sharing time at the qasgiq. The evening sharing time is when we bring our extra food that we stored to share with the village families. Since each family shares their own food with the potlatch attendees, we use this opportunity to replenish the food supply that was used by each family. We use this quiet time to take a much-needed afternoon nap.

Darkness is beginning as we bring a sled to the front of our cabin to load it with the food that we will share during the sharing time at the qasgiq. Every family in the village will also share their extra food with other families in the village. This is our way of helping each family replenish the food that was needed to feed the attendees that stayed with each family. We don't want any family to have a food shortage because of the potlatch.

Rather than hitching our dogs to the sled, we attach the tow rope to the sled and pull it ourselves. The dogs are puzzled by why we are pulling the sled and not using them. In their canine brain they must think we humans are a strange kind. It is a short walk to the qasgiq anyway; why bother with the dogs. They bark their disapproval as we leave.

We stop at grandpa's cabin so they can join us as we all walk to the sharing event. It is a wonderful sight to see all the sleds full of food to be shared parked outside the qasgiq as we arrive. Even the three schoolteachers bring food items to be shared.

When everyone in the village is settled in the communal house, grandpa explains the process used to distribute the food. After he explains the distribution, he thanks everyone for a wonderful potlatch. He is proud of how everyone contributed to its success.

As grandpa leaves the fire pit, Robert, one of the teachers, steps next to the fire pit to announce that missionaries from the church in Mamimuit will soon be here to speak to the group. Robert explains that the missionaries are bringing games for the children of all ages to participate in during the night's address. They are bringing enough games to give to each child as a take-home gift.

As grandpa walks back to our group, Pa confronts him and with a very distressed look asks grandpa, "Did you know about these missionaries coming to our Kagemuit potlatch?" Grandpa says, "It is the first I heard of it." "I am not happy with this announcement!" Pa says with a voice that Ma hears. Ma takes Pa aside and explains that he should not show his anger in front of the villagers and teachers. Ma has a way to calm Pa's anger, and he calmly tells her, "We will not stay for this. I am not going to be lectured to by a bunch of white men that do not understand our native ways." Pa calmly tells Ma. "We don't need to stay, and I will tell our family that we are going home," says Ma. When Kuvak and Algaq hear Ma say that everyone in our family is going home right now, they object. "The missionaries are bringing games for us to play and take home," says Kuvak. "I want to stay also," adds Algaq. Grandma overhears our argument and says that she and Apak will stay with the children. "They really want to play with the other children," Grandma speaks in her reassuring tone. "It will be very late when the games are over," Pa adds. Grandma states, "They can stay with us for the night, since it will be very late when the games are finished." "Okay," says Ma to grandma. "They will be just fine, don't worry about them," states grandma in her reassuring tone.

Just as we leave the qasgiq, we see the group of missionaries parking their sleds near the dog sled hitching area. By the time we enter the cabin, Pa is no longer angry, and he places a pot of water on the stove to heat for coffee and tea. Kenruk remarks to me, "I have never seen your Pa that upset." I explain to Kenruk that Pa feels strongly about our native heritage, and he does not tolerate anyone attempting to undermine how he feels about that. Pa does not agree with the missionaries' attempt to convert the Eskimos to their religion. Pa knows in his heart that there is a supreme being responsible for creation. But he will embrace those thoughts on his own. Anngaq settles into his corner of the cabin with a book and Nayagaq shares fresh bread with everyone. We are all tired from the day's sharing and get ready to retire for the night.

Chapter 11

It has been an exciting weekend of potlatch activities. As always, Pa is up with the fire going and heating water for coffee. Anngaq and Nayagaq are attaching their dance fans to the cabin wall. They get to add their fans to the other fans from the family's first dances. Nayagaq places her dance fans next to mine, with Anngaq hanging his fans next to Nayagaq's fans.

It is sunrise by the time we all wake up. No need to get up early. We have no outdoor plans today. We just sit around the cabin relaxing. It will be a day of rest. We wait for Kuvak and Algaq to come over from their overnight sleep at grandpa's cabin. We wonder what games they will bring that were given to them by the missionaries.

Ma begins preparing the noon meal. She asks, "Why haven't we seen the children yet?" "I thought they would be here by now to show us the games they received," Nayagaq adds, wondering why we have not seen them. "Qataruaq, go over to grandpa's cabin and have the children come over for the noon meal," Ma orders. "I will," I answer while I put on my parka and other winter clothing.

It is another clear and cold day as I open the cabin door and step outside. I walk over to grandpa's cabin. The entire village seems very quiet today. Everyone is probably resting after a late night at the qasgiq. No one is outside. It feels very strange throughout the village.

I open the door to grandpa's cabin, and I am greeted by Kuvak as he gets up from his sleeping blanket in the corner of the cabin. "I don't feel good, Qataruaq," he says with sweat beading on his forehead. "How do you feel?" I ask. He replies that he feels hot, with a sore throat and a headache. I go over to Algaq, and she has the same condition.

I turn my attention to grandpa and grandma. They are almost motionless laying in their bed. Their breathing is very labored and difficult. I am startled by the color of their skin that looks unusual with a blue, black color. Something is very wrong with them. I cannot get any response when I talk to them and try to shake them. I tell Kuvak and Algaq to stay here while I go get Ma and Pa. They are in no condition to walk and lay back on their blankets. I hurry and run to our cabin.

I quickly open the door and tell Pa, "There is something very wrong with grandpa, grandma, and the kids." "What's wrong?" is Pa's reply. "The kids don't feel good, and grandpa and grandma are almost lifeless in their bed." "Go to the school and get Emily so she can check on them," Ma says. Pa tells me, "Go and run as fast as you can to get Emily."

I still have all my winter gear on as I close the door and run to the school building. Upon entering the school, it is eerily quiet. No children are in class and Emily is making a soup for her noon lunch. "Where are the students?" I ask. "No one came," is her reply. "What brings you here?" Emily asks. I tell her that my grandpa and grandma are very sick and are not responding to me. Kuvak and Algaq have a fever, sore throat, and a headache. "Since I have no students, we should go and see what is wrong," she says. We both waste no time and run to grandpa's cabin.

When we arrive, Ma and Pa are crying and tell us that grandpa and grandma are dead. The children are very sick. Their breathing is very labored, and they are bleeding from their nose. Emily enters and goes right to the children. She notices their skin has turned blue. She looks over at the lifeless bodies of Apak and Emak. "What is going on, Emily?" ask Ma and Pa together.

"I don't know. I have never seen anything like this before," she says. "I need to hurry back to the school building and call the hospital in Anchorage for their opinion regarding what we can do," Emily responds as she rushes out the door. I follow behind her as we run to the school building. I do my best to keep up with her. She is a very fast runner.

As we approach the nurse-aid door of the school building, we see almost the entire village waiting for her. Everyone looks ill or very ill as they sit next to her door. "It looks like we have an acute health emergency, and I am going to contact Anchorage hospital to get their opinion as to what I should do," she tells everyone. She asks for everyone's patience while she makes the call.

Emily returns from her call and tells everyone that there is a territory-wide health emergency that describes the symptoms you are experiencing. Unfortunately, there is no cure according to their doctors. "My only advice is to go back to your cabin and do not interact with anyone. I am sorry, but that is the only comfort that I can give you at this time," she states with an apologetic frown in her expression. She also includes that there are reports from many villages to our south and west that are experiencing sudden sickness leading to deaths.

I run back to grandpa's cabin. When I enter, I see the unbelievable. Ma is holding the lifeless body of Algaq, while Pa is putting Kuvak on the blanket and covers his lifeless body. "They died so suddenly," they both say. "There was nothing we could do to save them," Ma explains. "Their breathing became so labored as they gasped for breath," Pa explains. "We simply watched them take their last breath and die," Ma says with her tears taking the place of her words.

I explain what Emily learned from her call to the Anchorage hospital. I tell them that we are experiencing the same sickness and death as the villages to our south and west. This has been expanding into our area for the past several months. She says the best way to prevent getting sick is to stay in our cabin and not interact with others.

Ma asks Pa, "How do we handle the bodies?" Pa states that we can't bury them because the ground is frozen with packed snow covering it. "This sounds uncaring, but should we just place them on the roof?" I suggest. We all agree that we can't leave them in the cabin. With all of us in agreement, we go over to grandpa's cabin and place the bodies on the roof. As we lift the bodies of Kuvak and Algaq, we notice the game boxes that were given to them by the missionaries next to their blankets. With all four bodies placed on the roof, we know in our hearts that this is the best we can do for them as we wrap them in blankets taken from the cabin.

We turn our attention toward Kevig's cabin and notice the bodies of Ukurraq and two of his children have been placed on the roof. We look around the village and every cabin has some bodies placed on their roof.

We heed the warning issued by Emily and return to our cabin, so we do not interact with anyone. It is now getting dark as we go inside.

Hardly a word is spoken as Pa prepares the fire to heat water, and Ma prepares our evening meal. While we are eating, Nayagaq asks, "What are we going to do, Pa?" Pa replies, "It appears that we are the only healthy ones in the village, and I am considering leaving so we do not catch this sickness." Anngaq agrees, "I do not want to die." "What about you, Kenruk? You just watched your mother and your two sisters being placed on the roof. Your Pa did not look very healthy as he struggled with the effort." "I think you are correct that we should leave," agrees Kenruk. Pa asks me what I think. I respond that I agree with Pa. It appears that a sickness that no one understands has infected our village. Many people in our village are dead because of it. Because we cannot avoid this death if we stay, I think we should leave soon. Tomorrow may be a good time to leave. Everyone agrees and we begin to make a plan about how we depart. We all go to sleep wondering how many of our villagers will die tonight.

As usual, Pa is the first to wake up and restart the fire. He places the water pot on the cookstove to make hot water for coffee. Ma is making pancakes using the sourdough starter she received from Hungaq. It is a solemn time as we are very sad and having difficulty keeping from breaking out with tears from all the death that we had to experience yesterday. Pa is very quiet in his world of grieving for his Ma and Pa.

Apak was his personal leader in his life and his death has hit Pa very hard. The person responsible for his living the Yupik way is no longer available to answer Pa's personal questions about life's difficulties. Now is when he needs him most, but he is gone from his life. He has lost two of his children but has no one to comfort his grief. He now faces the certain reality that he must leave Kagemuit behind and search for a new home in a place unknown. If his family needs his strength, it is now.

Ma is having her own difficulty trying to cope with the deaths of Kuvak and Algaq. As the youngest children, they were precious "little ones" as she often called them. Their youthful energy that filled our cabin is gone. The silence inside these four walls is deafening. I know she is grieving so much, and no words that I can offer can change any of that. Only time will heal that pain and hurt of a broken heart.

I can't determine how Nayagaq and Anngaq are handling their grief. They understand that they must leave the only village they have ever known. They must not only grieve the loss of their cousins but set their thoughts on living in a place where they can only imagine what it will look like. Both add to the silence within the cabin as they do not want to be the first to speak. What can anyone really say that will change what we have just experienced?

Kenruk breaks the silence and says that he wants to go to Kevig's cabin and determine how his Pa and Qilak, his sister, are doing. "I have to go and look into their situation," Kenruk's words echo within the cabin, although he fears the visit will not end well. I agree as Kevig did not look good when we watched him place his dead on his roof. I tell Kenruk I would accompany him for emotional support. We both leave the cabin fearing the worst but hoping for a miracle.

We walk over to Kevig's cabin, and we already feel the silence of the place. There are no voices to be heard. Kenruk opens the cabin door and immediately begins to cry as all we see are the lifeless bodies of his Pa and sister. All we can do is wrap them in blankets and place them on the roof beside his wife, son, and other daughter. "This is the most difficult thing I have ever done in my life. I hurt so much," he says with his face covered in tears. "The hardest part of living is the dying of our loved ones," Kenruk says as a philosophical end to those he loved so much. We quietly return to our cabin. The death from this sickness never stops, as I think in my head.

We are discussing our plans to leave when Emily enters our cabin. She seems to be very healthy and not affected by the sickness. She wants to come by to see how we are doing. She notices that we are all healthy and unaffected. Emily explains that she thinks this is what she calls a pandemic that has spread to the lower river area. I have no idea what she means by the word pandemic and really at this time don't care to know. Her thinking is that the missionaries from Mamimuit may be the carriers of the sickness. Everyone, including us teachers, took part in the potlatch during the first two days. Only our family and her and Janet did not stay during the time the missionaries were present. Everyone, including Robert, stayed to listen to them speak and interact directly with them. These are the ones that have been infected. The ones who did not stay included our family and Emily and Janet, who did not catch the illness. Robert died last night. "I radioed the Northern Commercial store to have Janet and I removed from here this afternoon with their company's dog teams," she says. I ask Emily, "What did you do with Robert's body?" "We wrapped him in the school's blankets to bring him back to Mamimuit and eventually to his home in Idaho," she says. I express to her how Robert had become a good friend of mine. She knows that Robert really enjoyed the time he spent with us and our family. "All of you were very special to him. He talked often about how he desired to learn from all of you regarding your Yupik ways." Emily asks Pa, "What are you going to do now that all your brothers' and sister's families have died with this sickness?" Pa states that he is going north to escape to a river up there. "It sounds like another big adventure awaits you. I wish you the best," Emily responds. "I should leave now to wait for the store's dog teams to arrive soon." We all give her a hug as she leaves our cabin and thank her for the good work she has done for our village.

Pa tells us that it is time to put our plan together. Kenruk goes to his Pa's cabin to bring back Kevig's dog team. We will leave with three dog teams with one sled in tow to carry supplies. Pa advises that we need to take enough dried fish for ourselves and the dogs. We bring our nets and ice picks to catch fish when our supply runs low and needs to be replenished. Our guns and ammunition are required anywhere we go. We take with us as much food and provisions that we can carry along with our cookware. Tarps, blankets, and extra clothing are taken with us. We make room in the extra sled to carry our snares and traps to use at our new home wherever that may be.

We hitch our three dog teams to the sleds and take off. Just like that, the only home I have ever known is behind me. We head to the slough and notice that the roof of Qavcik's cabin only holds four bodies. We realize that someone is still in the cabin. We stop our sleds and Pa and I walk across the footbridge to her cabin and find Cakiraq's lifeless body inside. Pa wraps a blanket around him, and we lift his body to the roof with the rest of his family. I ask Pa, "What about her dogs?" He immediately goes to each dog and unhitches them from their doghouse, so they are free to go wherever they desire. He enters the smokehouse and we both throw out all the fish onto the snow for them to eat. We leave the smokehouse door open in case the dogs want to use it for shelter. We hope they find a way to survive.

As we walk across the bridge, we see Kiak with Arlunaq's dog team enter the river and head upriver. We assume she is going back to her home in Chagemuit. I guess that means that Arlunaq is dead from the sickness. Obviously, she did not get infected. It must be the half upriver Indian blood that kept her safe. "She is a strong woman," Pa says. "I am going to miss our annual trips to her moose camp," I say.

Pa and I take our places in the sleds and enter the river and head downriver. Shortly, we meet the Northern Commercial dog teams coming our way to take Emily, Janet, and the body of Robert back to Mamimuit. We are on our way to a destination that is not yet known, nor how long it will take us to get there.

Chapter 12

Pa and Ma lead the way using Pa's sled and his dog team. Kenruk and I follow next with my sled using Kevig's dogs. Anngaq and Nayagaq use Anngaq's sled with the mixed group of dogs that Pa received from his brothers' and sister's teams when Tungay left to go back to Mamimuit. I tow the extra sled. The dogs eventually settle into a pace where the world around becomes quiet. The only sound is the feet of the dogs and the sled runners sliding over the frozen river.

I wonder what the six of us are thinking as we make our way downriver. We seem to be going to a place we do not know and will recognize it only when it finds us. Kevig's dog team is not running as a team and is straying from their line and constantly tugging at their rope they are tied to. I pull our sled up to Pa and tell him the dogs don't seem content with their position in the team. Pa looks at each dog's behavior for a while as we run next to him.

After Pa has time watching each dog in the team, he raises his hand as a signal to stop. Pa repositions some of the dogs, and before we start again, he tells Kenruk to drive the sled and see if that helps. The team may behave better with a driver they recognize. Kenruk has run this team before without the dogs behaving as they are. I get into the sled basket while Kenruk does the driving. The team now runs in unison with the new arrangement and Kenruk as the driver. Pa demonstrates his excellent dog management skills.

Evening is soon upon us as we see the village of Kwigamuit ahead. We pull our sleds next to Pa and discuss what we should do. Ma wants to stop if we do not see any bodies on the roofs of the cabins. We remember what Emily warned us about interacting with anyone. "Maybe the missionaries did not stop here," I say. We all decide it may be safe to stop and visit for the night. As we come near the village, we do not see any bodies on the roofs. "I think it is good to stop," says Pa and Ma quickly smiles in a show of her approval.

We stop our sleds in front of Ma's brother's cabin. We are greeted by their two children with hugs to Ma. Taruq and Hungaq come to the door. Taruq greets us with a puzzled look and asks, "What a surprise to see all of you. What brings you here during the evening?" Ma immediately asks, "Is everyone healthy and doing fine?" "Yes, we are all healthy. Why do you ask?" is Taruq's reply.

Ma explains the sickness that occurred after the potlatch ended. She advises them that we are the only survivors of the sickness, except for Kiak who left for her home village upriver. We placed all of the dead bodies on the cabin roofs and fled as quickly as possible. "They are all dead?" they ask. "Yes," is Pa's reply, hardly able to contain his emotion. Taruq asks, "Where are Kuvak and Algaq?" "They died from the sickness along with Apak and Emak," Pa explains. They respond that they are heartbroken to hear this news.

They invite us for coffee, and we accept. We talk while having coffee and pilot crackers. The entire village of Kagemuit is vacant as everyone died with the sickness that we think was brought by missionaries during the final night of the potlatch. "No missionaries have stopped by as we rarely get any strangers," explains Taruq. "That explains why everyone is healthy and has not been exposed to the sickness," says Ma.

Taruq tells us that his parents' cabin is still not occupied, and we are able to use it for the night or as long as we need to stay. We accept the offer. We need to take care of the dogs as they are down by the river. "You can tie them up to Pa's smokehouse and use the straw to bed them," he says. With the dogs bedded and the sleds brought to the cabin, we prepare to sleep for the night. It is an unexpected pleasure to sleep in a cabin as we thought our night would be spent sleeping along the river out in the open.

The next morning, we walk over to Taruq's cabin. They have hot water heating for coffee while Hungaq is making sourdough pancakes. Taruq breaks the silence and explains that he has consulted with his brothers and sisters, and they want to convince us to stay with them in the village. We are welcome to live in their parents' cabin. They explain that Kwigamuit is a good fishing location. Trapping and berry picking are located close by. They all agree that they would be happy to have us live with them. Their village could use an experienced wood builder like Pa. Taruq gives us many reasons why we should choose to settle in their village. Taruq asks Ma, "Will you choose to stay with us?" Ma replies, "That decision is for Unozroak to make." Ma states that wherever Pa goes, that is where I will find myself. "What do you say, Unozroak?" Taruq asks.

Pa answers that he is just like his Pa, in that he wants to start a new beginning. His Pa established a new settlement that became Kagemuit. Pa wants to establish a new settlement and now is his opportunity to do so. "I want to be my own person, living in a place that is of my choosing that I feel is good for my family," Pa says with the strength of an elder that he is. In addition, Pa adds, "This is the time that has been given to me, and I plan to use it wisely." He knows the journey to accomplish that dream is not known, but his family is the strength to see it happen. "I am all that is left of my Pa's family in Kagemuit and I intend to carry on his legacy," says Pa with his proud voice to everyone in the cabin. I look around at the members of my family and all of them nod their heads in approval. Pa turns to me and asks, "Qataruaq, do you agree with me?" I stand with boldness and say, "I will be with you wherever that journey leads me." Taruq then stands and with some disappointment in his voice says, "Then, Unozroak, you have our blessings and encouragement as you proceed on your journey." "Thank you," is the simple answer in reply given by Pa. Taruq indicates that he will provide any help that we need during our journey. Pa replies that we have all the provisions that we need.

Before we walk to our sleds, Ma wants to go to see the graves of her parents. Taruq leads us out the door and we walk toward the village cemetery. Her parents' graves are easy to find as they are the ones with fresh dirt shoveled over the plywood coffins. The winter snows made an igloo-like dome over the coffins. The coffins are about halfway buried into the permafrost before the cold stopped the process of burial. Taruq explains that he hopes to have the plywood coffins completely buried by late spring when the soil warms to continue his digging efforts. Ma says, "The white crosses are very well made. They represent the beauty of their lives."

We turn and head back to Taruq's cabin where we find that Kenruk has the three dog teams ready to go. By this time all of Ma's brothers' and sisters' families have gathered to wish us goodbye. After giving and receiving many hugs and well wishes, we mount the sleds and head toward the river. As we go down the riverbank and make our turn downriver, we all turn and give our farewell wave to everybody standing on the riverbank. They all wave back. I think to myself that I will never see these people again that were a big part of my life. I can only imagine what Ma is thinking right now. She seems completely in agreement with Pa's decision to move on. I also wonder what each of the people standing on the riverbank must be thinking about our future and why we would want to make such an adventure into the unknown.

We enter the portion of the river that widens, and if we were in our kayaks, our speed would slow. We encounter fewer pressure ridges, but we keep a keen watch for them so we do not come upon one unaware. Since we go much faster in our sleds than by kayak, we see Mamimuit in the distance. As we get closer to the village, we pull our sleds next to Pa and ask him if we will stop to see Tagneq at his store.

With our question, Pa raises his hand as a sign for us to stop. He says that we are not going to stop. Before we have time to ask why, Pa explains that he fears the sickness could be widespread in the village. He does not want to risk being exposed while visiting his youngest brother. He reminds us that he is still upset with the missionaries from the Kagemuit experience. The church is very close to Tagneq's store. He wants to avoid any contact with the church building and especially the missionaries. I want to see Tungay one last time. I will have to be happy with the memories that I have of our time together.

As Pa completes his explanation, we pick up our sled brakes and continue down the river. I have never been below Mamimuit on the river. This is an undiscovered country for me.

Only grandpa and grandma have been below this point. They used to live in a village far below Mamimuit before the tundra raiders forced them to leave. I have often thought about their journey to escape the death, destruction, and stealing by the tundra raiders. I can't imagine how life would have felt to live under those threats all the time. They could come without warning. I would fear for my life every time they occurred.

Now the greatest fear is surviving this territory-wide sickness that covers all sections of the lower Kusquqvak River. Are we going into the heart of the sickness? None of us knows the answer to that question. We must be careful with our contacts.

The journey now is uneventful. Endless tundra wherever we look. This is my kind of country. Wide-open spaces without trees to make me feel closed in. The dogs are running well at a steady pace. It is cold outside as we sled with our winter gear. Our fur hat, parka, mittens, and mukluks are essential to keep us warm as the sleds' speed creates a significant cold that our bodies feel. The daylight is starting to diminish, so we look for a place to stop and set up camp. We find a site that has some riverbank that will give us some shelter.

We position our sleds to make a four-sided appearance that will support our tarps with poles we find on the shore. We have a good roof, and the sleds provide our walls with a slight opening for us to enter and exit. Nayagaq is our fire maker with Kenruk scavenging for available firewood. We melt snow to make water for coffee, and Ma finds some dried fish for our evening meal. Anngaq and Pa cook fish for the dogs so they have a good meal to end our first day. I cut a few snow blocks to enclose any openings in the sleds to keep the wind out. Our improvised igloo works well to keep us sheltered, warm, and dry. We end our first day wrapped in blankets for a night of sleep.

We wake up with Pa making fire and melting snow to provide water for the morning drink. We each have a pilot cracker with shortening. It is a quiet morning as each of us reflects on our journey ahead. How many mornings will we have? I think there will be more than I can count in my Yupik language. We each find our job at taking down the camp. Once we load the sleds, Anngaq and Pa hitch the dogs to each sled, and we depart for our second day of our journey.

By midday we encounter small islands in the river with sloughs that empty their water into it. These sloughs and small islands create pressure ridges that we need to be concerned about. The further we go, the fewer islands we see, but they are much larger. We stop at one of the largest islands as it has a lot of driftwood for fire making. It is nice to stop and have a hot cup of coffee. The island is covered with fox tracks and rabbit tracks. This is the last island that has significant willows for rabbit cover. The reason they concentrate here. Pa and I grab our guns and look for a rabbit that we can add to our evening meal. Rabbits are very concentrated here as they were upriver this winter. It is easy to catch a couple with our guns. We see evidence of many rabbits killed by foxes, leaving only their fur and bones behind. We return to our sleds and show Ma our catch. She is very happy to have them for our evening meal.

When we return, the fire is out and the pots and cups are washed and stored away. As we pass this island, the river doubles in size. We are surprised by the size of the river now. We have never seen one this wide. We stay near the edge of the river to avoid any pressure ridges that are sure to develop in the middle. There are no islands as we go further down the river. It is complete monotony as time passes. It becomes twilight and we decide to camp for the night. Rabbit for our evening meal sure sounds delicious.

The next morning brings a beautiful but cold day. We use all our cold weather gear just to stay warm. Our breath creates a thick fog before each of us as we speed down the river. I think how my life has been very rewarded to have a Ma that is so good at skin sewing to make clothing to protect us from the severe cold that we experience today. The dogs are even happy to be able to wear dog coats and booties that Ma made for each of them. A warm and dry dog is a happy dog and will work harder because of Ma's help.

It warms a little as the sun rises. The river continues to widen the farther we go. We come upon an abandoned village to our right. We are curious about its origins and demise. While we walk to the remnants of the cabins, Pa indicates that this place is very similar to the one that Apak and Emak described to him. "The very large cemetery surrounded by four mud houses with crosses on the top is just like the one Pa described to me," Pa says. The cemetery is one of the largest he has ever seen. Its size was due to the many deaths caused by the tundra raiders that grandpa and grandma fled.

We think it has been about thirty years since grandpa and grandma left this village. Many of the crosses in the cemetery have almost disappeared into the permafrost. We consider the thought that either grandpa and grandma's parents and relatives are possibly buried here. I am humbled by the thought that my great-grandparents likely walked this tundra.

We turn away from the cemetery and walk towards the cabins. I imagine that one of them could have been my grandparents' cabin that we are visiting today. We are unable to open most of the cabin doors because they have sunk too deep into the permafrost. The few that have lost their door show us mostly empty dwellings. A few drying racks still stand as a testament to a once thriving fishing community. One of the drying racks that has fallen to the ground still holds an old torn fishing net still attached. We spot a beluga whale gut buoy hanging from an outside cabin wall. Beside each cabin is a smokehouse exhibiting various stages of decay. Some are only recognizable as a pile of wood. I stand in awe of this place and try to picture it as my grandpa would have seen it living his life as a young boy playing on the tundra. Then he becomes a mature married man with grandma by his side.

We turn and head to our sleds as the dogs are becoming restless and our bodies are getting cold. The dogs continue to run at their comfortable pace as we head into another twilight. We look for a good campsite and stop for the evening. We think the ocean is not far downriver.

This is our fourth morning since we left Kagemuit. The river becomes so wide that we feel that we must be at the place where the river meets the ocean. We look to the west and only see sea ice. We come across a local man tending his net. We stop and talk to him. He seems healthy and not affected by any sickness. We assist him while he pulls his net to see what he has caught. It yields a large catch of sheefish and whitefish. They are very large by our standards. The man tells us that these fish are fresh from the ocean, which explains why they are larger than the ones we catch.

We help him reset the net under the ice. After the net is repositioned, the person thanks us for our help. He gives us some of his catch and we thank him for the generosity he provides. We ask him where he lives. He indicates that his village is around the corner of the bay to the north. We tell him we are fleeing the sickness and want to go north to the big river. He tells us that the sickness has caused the death of many in his village, and he is trying to catch enough fish to feed his family and the few people that survived the sickness.

He asks, "You are going to the big river you say." "Yes," is Pa's answer. "Do you know the way?" Pa asks. He tells us that we need to follow the ocean to the north. That is all he knows about the route. We thank him for his generosity, and we depart to the northwest to begin our journey on land. It is nice to leave the Kusquqvak River behind and take our journey north.

Chapter 13

Our journey toward the big river takes us in a westward direction along the ocean coast. It is a land of flat tundra with what appears to contain hundreds or thousands of lakes and ponds. We stay close to the ocean coast. Since it is winter, we can use our dogsleds to drive on the tundra with relative ease. Any travel on this tundra without frozen snow would not be possible. It is a land of water and marshes.

The villages we encounter appear to have been very infected by the sickness. We want to be safe, so we approach each village cautiously. If we see no people outside, we conclude that we will not make a stop. The ocean coast begins to turn north. We begin to run low on our fresh frozen fish and decide that we should stop at the next river we encounter. That will allow us to set a net under the ice and try to catch some much-needed food.

The next river we come across is not a wide river, but we will give it an attempt with our net. There is a village located a short distance upriver on a slough that leads into the river. There are some people outside, so we think it may be safe to visit with them. We ask if the river will provide some fish. They tell us it will provide us with a good catch of fish. The village is more isolated, and I think that keeps it from being infected by people from the outside.

The elder, called Tegganeq, of the village invites us to stay in their qasgiq while we fish the river. We ask what village this is and what it is named. He tells us his village is called Qipneq, which means "bend" as the village is located on a bend in the river. The people are all Yupik Eskimo. We are invited to have an evening meal with his family. They treat us to dried salmon dipped in seal oil. We have never used seal oil before. I like it added to the dried fish. His wife, Nukaraq, has just made a batch of akutaq with salmonberries that they share with us.

We share why we are passing by their village on our way to escape the sickness that infected our village. Tegganeq is very interested in our journey and thinks it is very brave of us to embark upon it. He has heard of the big river, but that is all he knows about it. Tegganeq explains the village is located here because it was a good point to ambush tundra raiders on their way to plunder the villages to the south. Pa tells the history of his father that had to flee the same raiders. He fled upriver to settle our village of Kagemuit. Tegganeq has not heard of our village. It is getting late, and before we leave for the qasgiq, Tegganeq tells us he will go with us tomorrow morning to help set our net. He knows a good fishing site on the river that has provided a consistent good catch of fish. We thank him for his hospitality and the use of their communal house.

As we leave the cabin, we check on the dog teams and give them dried fish to eat. Most of the dogs are sleeping on the snow but are happy to have a nighttime meal. We gather our blankets from the sleds and walk to the qasgiq. It is a nice change to be able to sleep inside and be warm during the night. Ma adds that she is very happy to be able to sleep on something other than the cold ground.

After we finish the morning meal prepared by Nukaraq, we prepare our fishing gear and load it into Pa's sled. We look forward to catching many fish from the river. Tegganeq brings his dog team to meet us at the qasgiq. He admires Pa's dog sled and asks who made it. Pa explains that he makes all his sleds, kayaks, and fish traps for his use and for others. Tegganeq is curious about the wooden circle that forms the back of the sled. "That must require an experienced wood bender to make that circle," he says. Pa states that circle is his signature creation that he uses on all the sleds that he builds. "It makes them stand out from other sled builders," Pa says with pride that someone recognizes his work. "You are a very gifted wood worker," Tegganeq states with some envy in his words. "We could use someone in our village with such skills," he says. Tegganeq adds, "Our sleds are all passed down to us from previous generations and are becoming old and in need of repair." "Do you have wood strips that can be used to repair a sled?" Pa asks.

"Yes, but no one has wood bending experience," he says. "After we set my net, I can examine people's sleds and make repairs," Pa says. "The people would be grateful if you are willing to do that," Tegganeq says with a smile on his face. "I would be happy to teach someone how to bend wood and make repairs," says Pa.

With our sleds ready to depart, Pa and I follow Tegganeq down the slough to the river. We come to a bend in the river that Tegganeq says should be a good site to place our net. Each of us gathers an ice pick and begins chipping holes in the ice. The ice is not as deep as we have at Kagemuit. The ocean nearby keeps the temperature a little more moderate. With our holes made in the ice, we use our net pole to shove the net under the ice to the next hole to be pulled from the water. After the net is set, we take our sleds back to Qipneq.

At the qasgiq, Nayagaq is heating water for coffee and tea. Ma is washing clothes ready to hang outside to freeze dry. Pa explains that we may be here a little longer as the village people need his help repairing their sleds. Ma thinks that is a good idea as she could use a break from the dog sled life. Tegganeq comes by with a sled full of wood and a young man named Ayagyuaq that wants to learn wood bending skills. Ayagyuaq's sled certainly needs a number of sled pieces replaced.

Pa takes four pieces of wood boards to make a long box that he calls the bending box and cuts two pieces of wood to use as ends to enclose the box. Pa uses a hand drill to cut a hole in one of the boards near the end of the box. Pa asks for a tin can that he can use to hold water and attach it to the hole. Pa then explains that the piece of wood that needs to be bent is inserted in the box and the tin can is filled with water. The ends of the box are covered by the wood blocks and position the can filled with water over a fire to create steam to heat and saturate the wood piece inside the box. Pa tells Ayagyuaq this will prepare the wood for bending once it is taken out of the bending box. Ayagyuaq is impressed with the bending box that Pa gives him. Pa adds that a person must be patient as you make the bend. Do not force the bend or the wood will break. Experience will be your best teacher as you learn wood bending.

He is now ready to select a piece of wood that matches the piece of wood on the sled that needs to be replaced. He follows Pa's instructions to heat the wood piece. The wood will need to be heated for several hours before it is pliable for bending. Ayagyuaq is excited to be able to repair sleds in the future. "This will be a great help to the village as the sleds can now be repaired and new ones built," Ayagyuaq says in an excited voice. Tegganeq says, "Now our village can build and repair our sleds." You can feel the excited atmosphere in the qasgiq with this new skill that now exists in the village. Pa encourages Ayagyuaq by telling him that with experience he will become an excellent wood bender.

Tegganeq thinks it is a good time to check the net. As we approach the net, I notice that each hole is not completely frozen over. We chip away the skim ice and begin to pull the net. Tegganeq chose well as our net yields many sheefish and whitefish. We have enough fish for ourselves and have enough to share with the village. We place the fish that we keep ourselves in gunny sacks to freeze for later use on the trail. Many fish are given to Tegganeq to share with the people of the village.

We return to the qasgiq to find Ayagyuaq bending the wood so he can replace the worn piece on his sled. Pa tells him that he has done well and now he should be capable of working on his own. Ayagyuaq is so happy with his first successful wood bending that he gives Pa a very warm and long hug. "Your teaching has provided a skill that our village has long needed," he says. He attaches the newly bent wood piece and takes his sled outside to give it a trial run. Tegganeq wants to use the qasgiq tonight as a sauna night for the village. We all agree that it is very needed, especially for us.

We have an evening meal of fresh fish cooked by Nukaraq with Ma helping. Nayagaq makes bread for the meal this evening. Nukaraq says she does not make bread very often except for special occasions. While we have our meal, Tegganeq gives us some of the history of his village. As he mentioned earlier, this location was chosen because it was protected so that tundra raiders would come upon it without seeing it first. It made for a quick and complete ambush of the unsuspecting raiders. "They never knew what hit them until it was too late," Tegganeq says with pride in his voice. "We are completely isolated from anyone. That has advantages and disadvantages for living here. Our subsistence is dependent upon salmon during the fishing season. We also hunt seals that come into the river as they chase the migrating salmon.

"We get the chance to harvest beluga whales during the summer when we decide as a village to collect everyone together and try to catch one. It takes our entire village men to harpoon and bring one to the village. A whale will provide a lot of meat for our small village." He adds that a beluga will provide a large amount of muktuk or the fat that is the layer below the skin. They render the muktuk to allow it to turn into oil. The oil is used to flavor our food and can also be used as fuel in an oil lamp. Their cabin has many jars of oil on the shelves. Apparently, they use a lot of oil. It is exciting to listen to Tegganeq and Nukaraq talk about seal and beluga whale hunting as these marine animals provide for the many needs of their village.

Tegganeq informs us that it is time to go for a sauna. The men go first, so Pa, Anngaq, Kenruk, and I gather our towels and follow Tegganeq to the qasgiq. As we enter, the fire is already burning and it feels warm. Tegganeq introduces us to the men present. He recognizes Pa for his gracious teaching to Ayagyuaq of wood bending that will be a great asset to our village. The men thank Pa for his teaching wood bending that has been needed in the village for a long time. It is refreshing to have a sauna after many days on the trail. The men exit the sauna as the women including Ma and Nayagaq wait their turn to take a sauna.

We walk to the dog yard where we feed our teams fresh fish. They wag their tails in appreciation of a meal with fresh fish. Tonight, they get treated to straw that is provided by the village. I tell the dogs not to get too used to this treatment as we have a long way to go on the trail ahead without this luxury. As if they could understand my words. After everyone has taken a sauna, we think about retiring for the evening. We will have a good rest to conclude a very fruitful day of helping our fellow Eskimos.

The next morning Tegganeq enters the qasgiq to tell us he invites us to his cabin for the morning meal before we leave. He is afraid we might leave without his treating us to a final meal. As we enter his cabin, Nukaraq has completed her preparation of our meal. Ayagyuaq is sitting at the table happy to see us. Tegganeq tells us that the entire village is greatly appreciative of Pa teaching Ayagyuaq the wood bending skill. Pa says, "It was a gesture from me that I thought I should assist in any skill that I have to share." With that, we finish our meal and begin preparing for our journey.

As we depart with our sleds, the entire village sends us off with waves of goodbyes and words of gratitude. We head down the slough and turn onto the river with the ocean as our destination. The coastline leads us in a northerly direction.

Chapter 14

The journey continues to take us into unknown territory. We know that if we stay next to the ocean, it will eventually lead us to the big river. How many more days? We have no idea of the length of our journey. The unknown elements of time and distance make our journey wear on our minds. My mind wants to stay the course, but my body sometimes questions the whole idea. I know each one of us has the fortitude to accomplish this, but the mind creates uncertainty that can't be ignored. Each day we continue—stopping is not an option.

The days blend together as we fall into a routine of eating, sleeping, and running the sleds. The tundra landscape never changes, which begins to play tricks on our minds. Our nature desires a change of scenery just to keep our minds active. The monotony of the terrain and the whiteness of our surroundings makes it more difficult to keep the mind entertained with thoughts of persevering.

It is this whiteness that requires us to wear a mask to protect our face and eyes from the sun. This protection is mandatory, or we risk severe sunburn and eye damage. We make a mask-like device out of a piece of wood that we put over our face. It has two tiny slits cut horizontally where each eye can see out. Each person made their own mask to custom-fit their unique face and eye contour. Since these masks are personally made, the maker may add color to their individual tastes. Both Ma and Nayagaq have added color to their feminine look.

The mask also protects the face from frostbite. The cold tundra winds can lead to dangerous burns to the face and any exposed skin. The cold wind also has a way of numbing the brain. This numbness can lead to sleepiness if not watched for. A person can go to sleep on the sled because of this effect without realizing it is happening.

We came upon a large river—the largest one we have seen since we left the Kusquqvak. Pa stops to say this is a good time to use our net and catch more fish. It is a good time of day as it is still mid-morning. I think the dogs will enjoy a little rest to simply lay in the snow and enjoy the warm winter sun.

Ma and Nayagaq will use a pole with hook and line to try and catch some fish in the river. The pole is simply a willow branch that they find along the riverbank. They rarely get this opportunity to go fishing back in the village, and they seem very excited to get this chance. Kenruk is happy to chip their holes in the ice. Pa, Anngaq, and I work on chipping holes in the ice to set our net.

This seems to be a good fishing site, as the women are catching fish. Each time one of them pulls a fish through the ice, they are very animated with their voices of excitement. The fish are large, and it takes patience to pull them through the deep ice. Pa tells me, "It is good to see Ma having fun, as she is still grieving the loss of Kuvak and Algaq."

"This fishing opportunity is good for her mind," says Pa to me.

The net yields a good harvest of whitefish. The women's pole fishing catches ten nice-sized fish to add to the total catch. Pa thinks we have enough fish to allow us to continue our journey to the next river we cross for another fishing opportunity. It is late in the day, so we prepare for our evening meal of fresh fish. As Ma prepares the meal, she appears excited and very happy with her catch of fish.

Nayagaq tells me, "I have not seen Ma this happy and content with herself."

"Ice fishing did her a lot of good," Pa adds.

After the meal, Pa discusses our two options. "Should we follow this river to the northeast or follow the ocean coast?" Pa asks. "I don't know which to choose," Pa says.

I suggest we follow this large river as it may lead to a bigger one. It was just a thought, as I had no reason for my opinion. Pa states that it will be a change to river travel, which may be good for us. With that decision made, we position our sleds, cover them with tarps, and prepare for sleep.

Morning arrives with light snow falling. It creates a quiet environment as we try to ignore it and prepare to leave for a day on the river. We may find it annoying, but the dogs love it, and they are anxious to get on the river to run on smooth river snow. The ride is smoother than the clumpy tundra that makes for a rougher ride. The river leads to a large lake as twilight begins to herald another evening. The light snow has stayed with us all day. Our parkas and hoods are full of snow that needs to be shaken off. The dogs are also covered in white snow, but they are not bothered at all. Their thick fur kept them dry all day. We position our sleds as usual and cover them with our tarps. It will be a good feeling to finally be out of the snow for the night. The dogs quickly make a bed in the snow and go to sleep for the night.

The snow is falling heavier the next morning. We decided to ignore it and break camp for the upcoming crossing on this large lake to the north. The snow becomes heavier as we complete our lake crossing and enter a river to the north. The river meanders, and we see out of nowhere a village at a bend in the river. We don't see any evidence of the sickness, so we decide to stop and ask if we can find shelter to wait out the heavy snow that is now falling.

Our sleds catch the attention of children playing in snow forts, and they come to inquire about our arrival. They ask where we came from. I tell them we came from an upriver village on the Kusquqvak River. They have only heard of it from other passersby.

Adults from the village come to welcome us. They also ask where we came from. We explained the purpose of our journey, and then they invited us to their qasgiq. Their dwellings are all sod houses—they must not get any driftwood at this location. We are led to a very large sod house which I think is their qasgiq. It is nice to finally get out of the heavy snow as we enter. We find several men sitting around the fire pit having a discussion among themselves. We don't want to interrupt their discussion, so we quietly sit next to the entrance.

The men finish, and an older man comes to greet us. "I am Temyiq, the elder of Niugtaq, and I welcome you to our village," the elderly man says. He asks what brings us to his village. Pa explains our journey from Kagemuit is in search of the big river. He asks why we left our village. Pa further states that during the end of our potlatch, missionaries arrived, and our village nurse believed they carried a sickness that caused the death of our people. We fled to avoid receiving the sickness.

"You say missionaries may have been responsible for spreading the sickness?" Temyiq asks.

"Yes," was Pa's simple answer.

Temyiq states that his village has had problems with missionaries. He continued that they are forcing his village to stop having potlatches, Eskimo dancing, shamans, and using Eskimo masks during their dancing. "We were discussing among our men how we can resist their efforts. They want to take away our very way of life that makes us Yupik Eskimos. We must stand up to them, or else we will lose our identity," says one of the men leading the discussion.

"Our shamans are important leaders in this village. Missionaries want to silence them so they cannot speak to our people," the men complain. "The shamans are our spiritual leaders that we depend upon to guide us. If the shamans are banished, then we will have no one to guide us in the way that we must go. Just like an ayaruq helps the elder choose the right path to follow, our shamans help our village choose the right way to live. We cannot allow these missionaries to silence our shamans," said Temyiq with a very raised voice.

"If our people have no respect for our shamans, then we have no village anymore," said another man involved in the discussion group.

"They want us to stop having potlatches. The missionaries think our potlatches are a pagan celebration because we dance. They just don't understand the reason for our potlatch. Just because we don't believe in their God, they want us to stop. They don't want to consider that the purpose of our dancing is to perform and tell Eskimo stories," Temyiq explains the purpose of their potlatch celebration.

"They tell us not to wear our dance masks because they are an affront to their God. We tried to tell them our masks depict the story that we tell when we dance. Our masks don't encourage any belief in a pagan God—we tried to explain to them," added Temyiq. "How can we translate the story of our dance without a mask to tell the audience what our dance is about?" another man speaks up.

Pa says he understands the dilemma they face. "It sounds like the missionaries in this area are very strict and don't want to understand your concerns."

I thought it was time to speak up. I added, "I understand you are up against a religion that wants to assert itself without regard for your ancestral beliefs."

"You must stand up for your native roots, and I hope you prevail in your arguments," Pa adds.

After Pa made his statement, the men close their discussion. As each one leaves the qasgiq, they welcome us to their village. Temyiq asks how long we plan to stay. We tell him we hope to leave as soon as the heavy snow stops falling.

"We will allow you to stay in our qasgiq as long as you need. You can tie your dogs to our dog yard behind this building," Temyiq says.

Temyiq leaves, and Ma prepares our evening meal. We think about the discussion the men had regarding how to handle the concerns of the missionaries. Pa states his disdain for the missionaries that tried to convert him to their religion. Pa admits that he may believe that their God is the supreme being that he believes is responsible for creation.

"I just don't want them forcing their beliefs upon me," says Pa. "I want to figure it out myself in my own time," he further adds.

I tell Pa, "I believe you are correct, but it is hard to explain what you can't see or feel."

Everyone agrees with Pa and me. With the meal complete and dishes washed, it is time to gather our blankets and prepare for sleep.

As we went to our sleds to gather our blankets, we noticed the snow had stopped. We all help Anngaq with the dogs to feed them and move them to the dog yard. We feel the clear sky as the northern lights dance overhead. It already feels cold, and we quickly go inside the warm qasgiq. Tomorrow we are back on our journey north.

Chapter 15

We woke up to be greeted with clear skies, but very cold temperatures. We were ready for cold, but not a morning this cold. We use the fire pit inside the qasgiq to heat water for coffee and eat pilot crackers with shortening as our morning meal. As we exit the qasgiq, we are only greeted by our sled dogs ready for another trip. After placing our personal belongings in the sleds, we hitch up the dogs and take off. It is a quiet exit from the village with no one giving us a goodbye. We point our sleds north and continue the journey.

The ocean coastline provides our way on the never-ending tundra. We stay near the coast because it is less undulating and easier to handle our sleds. In quick succession, we cross three rivers as they empty into the ocean. We have a good supply of fish, so we decide not to stop at the first two crossings. When we encounter the third river, we decide to stop and try fishing with our pole and line. It may be a long time before we encounter another river.

"Better take this opportunity rather than risk it farther to the north," says Pa.

Kenruk finds willow branches from the riverbank so that everyone has a fishing pole. Pa, Anngaq, and I chip holes for everyone to fish. Our chances of catching fish increase with all of us having a line in the water. To each hook we attach a lure made from pieces of wood. The wooden lures are colored with a dye made from flowers and colorful plants that grow on the tundra in the summer. Ma and my sisters will collect them from the tundra near our village. The flowers were boiled to the point where the leftover residue has the color desired. The remaining dye is used to decorate the garments being made. These dyes are also used to decorate masks and the lures that we are using today with our fishing poles.

Our fishing effort is only partially successful. We do harvest enough to extend our food supply a few extra days.

"It is not what we were hoping for, but it is better than no extra food," says Ma.

We place our catch of whitefish in the gunnysacks and add them to our fresh frozen supply. There is still some daylight remaining, so we continue our northerly course along the ocean coast.

The next day out from our fishing in the river, the weather begins to change. Pa is concerned that it does not feel good. He knows a storm is coming our way from the ocean. His intuition proves correct as the sky darkens and a light snow begins to fall. The wind increases, and Pa decides to stop and prepare an igloo for protection. Everyone assists with the building of the igloo. Kenruk uses the snow saw to cut the snow blocks from the frozen tundra. Anngaq and Nayagaq carry the cut blocks to the igloo building site. Pa and I position the snow blocks to make the circular shaped walls and slope them near the top to make the roof. Ma helps to shield us against the wind the best she can. The wind makes it difficult to keep the snow blocks in the correct position without her help. The weather changes quickly with the wind blowing hard and the snow increasing in intensity.

By the time we cut and shape the final blocks for the roof, it is a full-blown blizzard. We position the sleds on the side of the igloo, and the dogs find their places in the snow and lay down as if it is just another night spent along the trail. Nayagaq starts a fire to warm up the inside and melt the snow blocks to seal the igloo interior. From the inside, Pa cuts a hole near the top to allow the smoke to escape. The high wind quickly sucks the smoke out of the igloo. Snow is melted for hot coffee and tea. We share dried fish for our evening meal.

We hear the wind outside as it creates a whistle effect around the igloo. It is very loud when the strong gusts blow. No sound from the dogs, as they are warm with a blanket of snow that has likely covered them. We have built a very durable igloo that should keep us well protected from this storm. We don't know how many days we will be stuck inside. A storm generated from the ocean could last longer than we desire. We must be patient—it is our way. Pa tells us that these spring storms can be violent and last for a long time. I hope that is not the case with this one.

The morning provides no relief from the storm. Pa makes a fire, and I go outside to quickly gather snow to melt for coffee. I am outside for only a moment but come back with my parka covered in snow. I shake the snow from my parka, but some land on Nayagaq, and she says to watch where I clean my parka.

I picked up a small bag that I brought inside the igloo and opened it to display its contents. Inside the bag is a piece of cloth with black and red squares drawn on it. There are also round wood pieces colored black and red. Pa asks me where I got this bag. I told him it was lying near Kuvak when I moved his body from his sleeping blanket to place him on the roof of grandpa's cabin. It must have been given to him by the missionaries during the final potlatch night of games for the children.

It looked interesting, so I put it in my pocket to bring it to our cabin. Nayagaq asks if I know how to use it. I reply, "No, but we can make up our own game." I arrange the red wood pieces on the red squares of the cloth and do the same with the black pieces and squares.

Nayagaq asks, "What do we do now?"

I think about it and suggest we move our wood pieces on the cloth squares of the same color and see what happens next. With only a few rules that I make up, we have a game that occupies our time while we are stuck in the igloo. Even Ma and Pa give the game a try.

Anngaq reads a book that he had placed in his parka pocket for just a time like this. Robert had given him the book as a Christmas gift from the school library. Kenruk asks what the book is about. Anngaq explains that it is a story about a dog named Buck that was stolen from its home in California. He is taken to the Yukon Territory where he is sold as a sled dog. He is part of a dog team that works during the Klondike gold rush.

"It sounds like an interesting story to read," Kenruk says.

"It depicts much of what we experience as we run our dogs," Anngaq says.

The storm continues for another day before it finally blows out. It is calming to no longer have to listen to the howling wind outside. Pa decides to wait until the next morning to set out to continue our journey. With a lull in the wind, we go outside to examine our situation. We notice the tundra has lost much of its snow from the wind. It has created bare spots that will make our sledding more challenging. The wind created a huge snowdrift on the side where the dogs are bedded. We move some of the snow to expose the dogs. They are still comfortable and sleeping. They were not affected by the blizzard.

"After every snowstorm, we have to endure the cold that follows," says Pa.

It is just the way of the north during the winter, I think to myself. All of us are busy moving our belongings from the igloo to the sleds. We hitch the dogs, and our journey continues. We don't go very far, and we come to a large bay, and we stay on land. The ice has lost all of its snow cover, and it is too dangerous to cross over it. We follow the curve of the bay, and we see large sand dunes to our west. We approach the sand dunes and realize that there are dwellings built into the side of them. The closer we approach, we see people outside, so we decide it is safe to go visit. Our curiosity leads us to one of the largest dwellings built into the dunes.

As normal, we are first met by the children's curiosity. Adults follow behind while an older man and woman come from the crowd to greet us.

"Welcome to Askinaghamuit. I am Taqukaq and this is my wife Maklak. What brings you here?" he asks.

Pa explains, as he always takes the lead, that we are on our way to the big river. Taqukaq knows about the big river and tells us that it is a several days' journey to get there.

It is very cold with the wind coming off the ocean as Taqukaq invites us to their qasgiq. As we enter the qasgiq, Taqukaq apologizes by saying, "I did not want you to stand out in the cold too long."

"You looked very cold from your journey across the tundra," he says.

Pa agrees, "It has been cold since the storm made us stop our journey."

He states, "That was a very strong storm that we got caught out in on the tundra."

I was surprised he did not ask where we came from. While Taqukaq makes a fire in the fire pit, he introduces himself as the village elder.

"You are invited to stay in our qasgiq to warm up and spend the night if you want," he says.

We took him up on his offer to stay for the night. Ma says, "I hope it warms tomorrow." In my mind, I hope she is right.

"You are welcome to have an evening meal at my dwelling if you want," he says.

Taqukaq and his wife leave, and we take the time to gather our dog teams. We take them to the dog yard and tie them up in front of the qasgiq.

We walked to Taqukaq's dwelling. It is a sod house built like all the rest into the large sand dunes. The entrance is built using driftwood logs to form a doorway. We enter and are greeted by Maklak cooking meat that I have never seen before. I ask her what this meat is that she is preparing.

She answers that it is tuntupiaq. I tell her that sounds like a reindeer that I have heard about. White people tried to teach the Yupik to herd them for money. It did not work as planned. She states that they are like reindeer, but these live wild on the tundra. "We go hunting for them each fall when the tundra turns colors. This was a good year to catch tuntupiaq, as each family has several to help with our winter food needs," Taqukaq adds.

Pa asks about the large sand dunes. Taqukaq tells us that they protect their village from ocean storms. He continues by saying that his ancestors began to use the sand dunes to build their homes. "If the sand dunes don't wear away, we are always protected from the sea. The violent ocean storms have worn down some of the dunes over time. Some of my people believe that someday the sand dunes will eventually disappear due to the continuing ocean storms that erode them with each storm," Taqukaq says, not certain if he believes that they might disappear.

I ask what fish are caught in the bay. He mentions salmon and halibut are caught from the bay. I tell him I don't know what a halibut looks like.

"It is a flat looking fish with both eyes on the top of its body," Taqukaq explains. He adds, "They can grow very large as they enter from the ocean. We also catch seal that swim into the bay," he adds.

After having the meat as our meal, Maklak serves us salmonberry akutaq. We thank them for inviting us and allowing us to stay in the village qasgiq for the evening. We also thank them for sharing with us the tuntupiaq meat.

Taqukaq walks with us to the qasgiq. He makes a fire for us as he explains that to the north there are large hills that will require us to go to the east and around them to continue our journey north. The ocean coast is too rocky to use for safe passage. The cliffs are too close to the sea and do not allow enough room to pass through.

"As you go around to the east and head north, you will see a mountain range we call Ingriller. When you see it, turn back to the west and follow the north side of the hills. This path will lead you back to the ocean. You do not want to travel in the tundra at this time of year, as the weather is starting to turn to spring. This is warming the permafrost and will make your journey much more difficult, if not impossible," he said. "The storm we just had has blown much of the snow from the tundra and will make your sled harder to run, so you want to stay close to the ocean," Taqukaq states with emphasis for our safety.

Pa thanks him for the directions around the hills. Taqukaq tells us to avoid the next village on the north side of the hills as they have been severely affected by the sickness.

"Sorry to hear that," Pa says.

"The risk is too great to stop and visit," Taqukaq informs us.

We retire for the night and wonder how the journey will go tomorrow with our detour around the hills. We all discuss the village with its unusual sod houses built into the sand dunes. These are people who have adapted well to the surroundings that they have been given to live with. Obviously, we have not seen anything like these large sand dunes, I thought. I wonder what would happen to this village if the sand dunes were washed away by the ocean storms. With those thoughts, we retire for the night.

Chapter 16

The new morning brought some relief with weather more suitable for sledding. The sky is clear and not as cold as before. It should be a nice day to continue our journey. We had just completed our morning meal when Taqukaq entered the qasgiq. He says that some of his villagers just arrived from fishing in the large lakes up northeast of the hills. He informed us that the tundra snow is melting and making for difficult sledding conditions on the north side of the hills. Pa says that it is good information to receive and helps us determine our route to the north.

Kenruk and Anngaq prepare the dogs, and we soon depart. The tundra conditions are good as we travel the south side of the hills. It takes us most of the day to reach the end of the hills to the east. Since the sun is moving north, we can travel in the shadow of the hills. This allowed us to put our face masks in our parka pockets. The sun begins to set as we make our turn to the north around the east end of the hills.

We make camp in the mildest conditions of our trip. It is nice to feel some warmth as we have our evening meal. The mountain, called Ingriller, is very prominent as the setting sun illuminates its westward slopes. The snow-covered mountain rises majestically from the flat tundra to the northeast.

Anngaq tells us there are Eskimo stories about how Ingriller came to exist. The story goes that a vole carried the mountain on its back and moved it there. When it leaned down with its hands, it formed the lakes next to Ingriller. Pa asks, "How do you know this story?"

"It was in one of the books I was given by a teacher a few years ago," Anngaq says.

"Do you believe this story?" Anngaq asks Pa.

Pa states with emphasis, "It is just an old Eskimo story of creation, and that is all it is."

As the morning breaks, for the first time in our journey we awaken with ourselves bathed in warm sunshine. We head west with the ocean as our destination. The hills are to our south and the open tundra to our north. The late spring blizzard we experienced seems to have changed the weather considerably for us. The sun is warming the tundra on this side of the hills. We begin to notice a very definite melting of the snow, creating a wet situation for the sled and dogs. The dogs have to pull harder because of the increased drag from the sled.

We encounter the ocean by mid-afternoon and make our turn to the north. The tundra is certainly beginning to melt. It is still snow covered, but it is not the cold dry snow—it is becoming wet and warm. The sleds don't slide as easily, so the dogs have to slow down and pull harder. My thoughts take me to how our progress has changed in just a couple of days. The weather is certainly becoming more summer-like. We knew this was going to happen eventually. I was hoping it would hold off longer.

I feel the slower we are going has made the twilight come sooner than expected. Pa signals to stop, and we move into our usual camp setup mode. Thankfully, there is enough snow to make the dogs comfortable, but it has noticeably lost much of its depth. The sun now sets more slowly as it circles the horizon to the west and drops out of sight. Ingriller, the mountain, is now directly east of our camp. We are farther away, so it does not appear as large as it was yesterday. I will go to sleep tonight and guess how the weather will affect us tomorrow.

A chinook wind developed during the night. It brought a warm wind from the southwest. We have only heard about these winds, as they did not occur in Kagemuit. These winds only melt the snow cover faster. The farther we go north, we encounter small sloughs that empty directly into the ocean. I notice that willows like to grow near the sloughs. I pull next to Pa's sled and ask him if we could stop at the next slough and try to catch a rabbit.

At the next slough that we encounter, we stop. Pa, Kenruk, and I grab our guns and walk toward a grove of willows. There is just enough snow to keep our approach quiet. Both the rabbits and ptarmigan are turning brown for the summer. They should be easier to see this time of year against the white background. From a distance, sitting outside some willows, is a rabbit enjoying the sunshine. Kenruk chooses to shoot first. It was a good catch as Kenruk demonstrates his shooting expertise. We take only a few more steps, and we find more rabbits sitting in the sun. All three of us take aim and catch three more rabbits.

Pa says, "That was easy."

I agreed and asked Pa if we need more. He indicated we had enough for now.

We walked back to the sleds, and Ma was very happy with our catch. "Those will make a very tasty evening meal," she said. We put the rabbits in the sled and continued our journey. The sledding became more difficult as the sun and the wind eroded the snow cover with more water appearing in small puddles. The dogs do not like the trail, and they must work harder as the day progresses toward twilight. The dogs needed a rest, and Ma wanted time to prepare the rabbits for our evening meal. We stopped early, resigned to a shorter day than usual.

"Conditions are deteriorating and making for difficult conditions on our sleds and the dogs," Pa says. We all wonder how many more days we have before we reach the big river. It was good to have rabbit for a meal, and we felt happy about that. It was dark when we finished eating, as we took our time and did not want to rush.

Just as we laid down to sleep, we heard raindrops on our tarps covering the sleds as our roof. I could see the disappointment in everyone's expression. I wondered what conditions we will face tomorrow. The dreaded rain has now arrived. Our journey has now taken a turn, and it is not for the better.

The rain continued throughout the night, and it was difficult to sleep. The rain falling on our tarps kept me awake most of the night. I knew worrying about it would do me no good. I was concerned about the conditions for sledding and its impact on the dogs, which have worsened. It was going to take longer to reach our journey's end.

A dense fog had moved in during the morning. The rain had stopped, but it was very misty outside. The fog and mist left a heavy feeling outdoors. It is the warmest morning we have experienced.

"Does the fog mean there could be open water in the ocean?" I ask Pa.

"It could mean we have either open water somewhere, or the tundra is becoming waterlogged," was his answer.

I really did not want to go outside because I feared the worst. But it was time to get the sleds ready for another day.

More snow had melted. The tundra was a mix of snow and green—some patches of snow and some patches of exposed tundra. At least we had some snow to help the glide on our sleds. I don't think the dogs will be happy. The dogs were very wet from the nighttime rain. As always, they were ready to pull the sleds. Rain or dry, they are always ready to go. The fog made for a very damp start of our day on the tundra.

As the sun rose higher in the sky, the fog began to disappear. It didn't make the going any easier, but we could see more clearly in the distance. I could only see the faint outline of Ingriller, the mountain. It was slow going with our sleds as the tundra conditions grew worse overnight, as I expected. We ran our sleds for a long time when we realized the dogs were getting tired and needed a rest. The farther north we go, the worse the snow conditions become. Pulling the sleds was really exerting and overheating the dogs.

We stop, and Nayagaq makes a fire to heat water from what little snow she could find. There were some willows surrounding small water ponds, and Kenruk and I decided to take our guns and try to catch some ptarmigans. Now that the ptarmigan has replaced their white feathers with brown ones, they again blended into their surroundings and became difficult to spot. Kenruk saw a couple standing on a small snow patch. He got my attention to their location, and we came away with a ptarmigan each. During our rest stop, we brought back to the sleds six birds to add to our evening meal. Ma was happy with our catch, as she desired a change in meals.

The dogs had rested and were tail-wagging ready to get going again. They wanted to pull the sled even if there was no snow. As we take off again, the sun feels warm on our face, and we no longer need our parkas, mittens, and fur hats. It did feel more comfortable not having to wear all the heavy winter clothing. There is a feeling of freedom without the need for all the clothing. The trek north continued at a slow but continual pace. Since we continue to encounter less snow, we are forced to not be able to stand on the sled runners but run behind. The person that was lying in the sled basket also got out and ran behind or to the side of the sled. This was good for the dogs, as it lessened the drag on the sled. We could go farther between each rest break. We still had no idea how far away the big river is.

Around mid-afternoon, we see a river in the distance. As we approach it, we notice that it is not our big river but one that needs to be crossed. As we arrive at the river's edge, we notice it is free of snow but covered in ice. The rain last night had melted the snow, which we assumed was normal. The ice only had a slightly white appearance. Pa thought it should be safe to cross.

We send Anngaq and Nayagaq across first in their sled. They cross without incident and stop their sled on the other side of the river. Kenruk and I take our turn crossing. We are pulling the supply sled loaded with most of our heavy gear. As we cross and approach the middle of the river, we hear and see a few cracks in the ice appear under our sled and especially under the heavier supply sled. This concerned me as we make it safely to where Anngaq's sled is stopped on the riverbank.

I dismount the sled and turn to alert Pa and Ma that we had some ice cracking under our sled when we crossed and they should choose a different approach to their crossing. They had already entered the river and were heading our way to cross before I could get their attention. They did not hear my warning. They appear to be making the crossing without any difficulty until their sled enters the portion of the river where the cracking occurred. Without any warning, the ice cracked with a loud sound. Their sled quickly entered the water with both Pa and Ma. The river current pulled their sled down into the water, and they were completely submerged under the broken ice. The strong current pulled the entire dog team underwater. We watched in horror as the dogs fought desperately to grab the ice with their paws to pull themselves out of the water. The current was too strong, and the submerged sled was being carried away in the underwater current. The dogs had no chance to fight the current, and they were all swept underwater. All that remained was broken ice among the open water.

We waited in hopes that we might see them surface among the broken ice. The surface of the ice was quiet with no sign of life. We looked with more hope that they would surface downriver from where they broke through. We saw nothing except frozen river ice.

"If I could have warned them before they entered the river," I said with tears in my eyes.

Nayagaq, with huge tears streaming down her face, said, "They're all gone—Ma and Pa, and all the dogs are gone."

The four of us stood on the riverbank and could not believe what we had just witnessed. I could not even stand as my legs buckled with my grief, and I fell to the ground. I kept thinking that this did not happen. It is a dream that I just had, and I will awaken from it. Anngaq just laid over his sled crying uncontrollably. Kenruk stood motionless in disbelief of what just happened.

"What do we do now, Qataruaq?" Nayagaq asks with tears still streaming down her face. My heart was breaking for the loss of her Ma, which meant everything to her. I wanted to give her some condolence for her grief, but all I could say at the time was, "I don't know." I tried to pick myself up from the ground, but there was no strength in my legs. Nayagaq just kept saying, "They're all gone, they're all gone." My mind was so numb. I don't know how long it took me to begin thinking about what to do next. The reality is that there was nothing I could do to change what happened. I tried to warn them, but it was too late. The river just took those that were so precious in my life. Even the dogs were like family to me. I lost them all.

Without my Pa, what do I do now? I kept repeating Nayagaq's words in my head. I am now the head of this family. I must find a way to be strong for those standing around me.

"We keep going north to the big river. That is what Pa and Ma would want us to do," I said to those standing next to me. I now found the strength to pick myself up from the ground.

Kenruk tells me that I am right. "Your Pa wanted this family to settle beside the big river, and that is what we are going to do," I said with confidence.

Nayagaq says in her sister voice, "But it hurts so much."

I walk to her and give her a hug that she so much needs.

Without a word spoken, we mount our sleds and head north. As soon as we leave, we come upon a village downriver as we head to the ocean. We simply go past, as we need to be alone. This is the time to be by ourselves. We don't go far before it becomes twilight, and we decide to stop and make camp. We each take up our own newfound job to setup camp and prepare the dogs for another evening. I get a sense that the dogs know that something very terrible has happened at the river crossing.

To give ourselves something to take our mind off the tragedy that just happened, we all work together at plucking feathers from the ptarmigans we caught for our evening meal. To break the silence while we work on the ptarmigan, Kenruk says to me, "Your Pa taught you everything you need to know. You just need to use the skills that he taught you." I knew Kenruk was correct, but it seemed so difficult to keep my mind at ease and to grasp the responsibility that I have just been given.

After our meal is complete and the dishes washed, we all try in our own way to find our individual peace. I walked outside to look to the southeast and look for Ingriller, as if it could give me any wise words. The evening is calm with the sun setting beyond the ocean to the west. I try to calm my mind as well. I look to the north and wonder how many more days it will take to reach the big river.

I enter our shelter, and Nayagaq raises her voice and directs her anger at me, "Why did we have to come to this place for my parents to die?"

"You know we could not stay in Kagemuit because of the sickness," was my reply.

"It hurts so much, and it isn't fair that good people have to die," Nayagaq continued.

"There is a reason for everything that happens, for good or bad," Anngaq breaks the silence.

I consider Anngaq's words and say, "You are right. We just don't know why things happen and the reason for them." It was getting late, and we decided it is time for sleep.

Just as the evening ended, the morning began with clear skies and a warm sun rising in the east. It was a beautiful beginning to our day as the rising sun makes a silhouette of Ingriller to the east. The dogs were awake and ready to unleash their energy to pull our sleds for another day. More of the tundra has melted. There is mostly water on the surface of the permafrost. Pockets of remaining snow on which to steer our sleds are few and far between.

The sledding is very slow as we are forced to use as much snow coverage as possible. The need for snow requires us to not be able to proceed in a straight line but must maneuver our sleds to places that have snow. The additional water that has appeared on the tundra is another hazard that we have to avoid. The water puddles and ponds must be avoided because they may become very deep.

The dogs know by instinct that they go toward the snow and avoid the water hazards. It is unavoidable that some travel on bare ground will happen. The dogs simply must work harder and use up more of their energy as a result. Since we can't continue in a straight line, we spend more time on the tundra to get from one point to another. The dogs are stressed not only by having to pull harder and longer, but the stronger sunshine heats their fur. The dogs stop at the larger water pools to get a drink.

The toll on our bodies increases as we must run with the sleds. We can't ride on the sled runners but run either beside or behind. With the hotter temperatures, we sweat heavily and soak our clothing. This becomes very uncomfortable and is not healthy when the sun sets and cools our sweaty bodies. Everybody is frustrated with these conditions—both dogs and humans. We both tire faster, and we don't cover as much distance. We must stop often because of these conditions.

I try to keep optimistic. The situation seems to work against us. I don't know how far away the big river is and how many more days it will take to get there. It is this unknown that plays on my psyche. I have to encourage everyone to be optimistic while I have my own doubts. I know we will ultimately get there, but how long will it take at the slow pace we must go? At each evening meal, the talk enters the uncertain and unknown phase of our journey. The trek works on everyone since our progress is so slow with the worsening tundra conditions.

One afternoon that seems like the many afternoons we have spent for the past many days on the tundra takes a turn that we all hoped for. Our northerly journey ends as the land turns to the east. Ahead of us is a big river as large as the Kusquqvak. I am in the lead sled this time and yell to Anngaq and Nayagaq behind, "I see the big river!" Their dogs sense my excitement, and they hurry their pace to pull Anngaq's sled next to ours. We stare almost with unbelieving eyes at the sight before us. The river is flowing full of moving ice from the river's breakup. We take this moment to give each of our party of four a group hug.

"We made it!" yells Nayagaq in absolute joy.

Chapter 17

Breakup on the big river is in full force. Large ice chunks float past, and we decide to continue our journey along the south shore of the river. We head our dog teams to the east and wonder where this will take us. The tundra is a saturated and water-logged combination of reindeer moss, dwarf shrubs, grasses, and lichens. Since we must walk our sleds, the going is difficult. The dogs don't like it either. We find it a little easier to travel near the river, but the ice bergs keep us from getting too close.

After a long, hard walk with the sleds, we see a large slough to our right. Down this slough we see many cabins.

Nayagaq shouts, "People! We might find people in the cabins!"

We are encouraged that the place that we have been seeking is before us. Twilight creates long shadows from the cabins that make up this village. Even from a distance, this village seems almost deserted. As we come closer to the edge of the village, we see dog sleds, but no dogs. I tell Kenruk that this is very strange to have no dogs.

We pass by each cabin that shows no evidence of being occupied. Only when we come near the last cabin in the village do we see an older woman standing in her doorway.

"Waqaa," she says as we recognize her Yupik hello to us.

I give her a "waqaa" in return. She seems to be very friendly as we come next to her cabin.

"I am Myack," she tells us her name in a welcome gesture.

I respond that I am Qataruaq. I point to the rest of our group and introduce Nayagaq as my older sister, Anngaq as my younger brother, and Kenruk as my cousin.

With the introductions complete, Myack invites us into her cabin. The interior is a very simple cabin with only the basic items for a meager level of comfort. It appears that she is the only one living in the cabin. She quickly asks while she is heating water for coffee, "What brings you to my village and where did you come from?"

I retell the same story that I have told every time I am asked this question.

She tells us that the sickness we escaped is the one that had decimated her village. She admits that the sickness has killed most of the people in her village. The few people that lived through the sickness remain in the village, but most women have lost their husbands. Many children have lost their parents. We finish our coffee as Myack tells us that Nayagaq can sleep in her cabin while the rest of us can sleep in her smokehouse. We thank her for her generosity and proceed to prepare the dogs for the night. Nayagaq takes her blankets and heads to the cabin while Kenruk, Anngaq, and I take our blankets to the smokehouse.

We step inside the smokehouse and see only a few dried fish hanging from the drying racks. I don't think she experienced a very successful fishing season unless there is another explanation for so few fish. On the wall hung a complete set of dog harnesses and towline. I did notice a sled outside the smokehouse. There was a kayak sitting on the roof of the smokehouse. Where are the dogs? The three of us roll out our blankets and get ready to sleep. I think as I lay in my blanket ready for sleep what happens next now that our journey has brought us to the big river.

We wake up as the eastern sun shows through the cracks of the smokehouse walls. Our first sunrise gleams off the big river water as it flows to the ocean. I reflect on the long journey that we experienced. So many experiences were entered into my memory. I never thought I would ever find myself standing on the shores of the big river. Where will the future find my life? Is this the end of my journey? What began as Pa's destination has now turned into mine. I don't think this is where my Pa would call his new home, but what about me? I ponder these thoughts until Kenruk tells me to come to the cabin for our morning meal.

Inside Myack's cabin, Nayagaq has the cookstove fire going and water boiling for coffee or my favorite, Labrador tea. Myack kept a supply in a jar that was ready for use. Nayagaq and Myack are enjoying each other's company. Anngaq joined the conversations between the two women. Nayagaq has returned to her old joyful personality. It was good to see her laugh and enjoy herself again. I think Anngaq has taken to Myack as he freely talks with her.

After the morning meal, Myack tells her personal story of the sickness and how it affected her. She tells us that about the time before they went berry picking, a ship stopped at their village carrying passengers from Seattle heading to Fairbanks. They were tourists wanting to experience Alaska. They stayed in their village only a couple of days, photographing their life in the village. One day after they departed, many people in their village came down with a terrible sickness. Many people died, especially the older people. Many men died of the sickness.

"I don't know why it selected mostly men," Myack said. "Even my husband and my son and daughter died because of the sickness," she said with still emotion in her voice.

Many parents died, leaving their children orphaned. The children have been sent to the orphanage at Akuluraq.

"Your village has been severely affected by the sickness," I said.

"Who remains in the village now?" Nayagaq asks, thinking the worst would be her answer.

She states that about a dozen women, but only two young men live in their village now.

I ask her what the name of this village is. She says it is called Nunam Iqua, which is Yupik that means "end of the land." That seems very appropriate, I thought, since it is located at the end of the river. She says the river is called Kuigpak, which means "big river." I began laughing at her answer, which she took as an insult. I apologized for my laugh because we never knew the name of the river that we were heading towards. I told her we always called it the big river, as that is all we knew about it.

She says that before people moved here to settle permanently, it was just a collection of individual fish camps. The people that live down the ocean coast from here would set up their summer fish camps at this location. The salmon that enter this river are very large and tasty. Eventually, her husband

and she decided to make this location their permanent residence year-round. Other families decided to do the same, and eventually a village of several cabins sprang up. By the time her two children were born, this village was a thriving subsistence community.

"Those were wonderful times with many memories," she said with a few tears beginning to fall from her eyes. "The sickness came and changed all of our lives," she continued.

I told her I know how she felt, as the sickness also devastated our entire village. "My youngest brother and sister died because of it," was my reply.

"It has been a terrible sickness that has invaded our territory," she said.

"During our journey, we have seen the great loss of life because of it from the Kusquqvak River to your Kuigpak River," I said.

"So many died so quickly that we had to dig a mass grave and buried everyone in it," Myack said.

I told her that our sickness occurred during the winter, and all we could do was place their bodies on the roof of their cabins.

"With the death of your older men and husbands, how has that affected your village since last fall?" I asked.

She said that it has been a very difficult time for the women. "Without our men to hunt and set nets under the ice to catch fish, we have reached famine proportions. We had exhausted almost all of our fish and fruit supply before the winter was only half over. We had to eat our sled dogs just to have something to eat." Myack explains that those were desperate times and they are not proud of the fact that they had to resort to such extreme measures.

"That explains the lack of dogs in the village," Anngaq adds to the conversation.

The two young men that survived are just too young and inexperienced to fish and hunt to help them provide food for the village. They were unable to provide for their subsistence way of life.

She also adds that with the loss of their men, they no longer have elders and shamans. "Without them in our village, we have no one that can give us wise words to live by," Myack states.

I agreed with her that every village needs an elder. An elder will lead the people, answer their questions, and give them Yupik guidance. It looks as though your village will be without an elder for some time in the future.

I try to give her some assurance and explain to her that we can help with the food shortage. "We will go hunting for food tomorrow from your nearby tundra. We need to meet the two young men that we can teach our subsistence ways of life," I told her. She will lead us to their cabin. They are brothers and live with their mother.

Myack leads us to their cabin. As we enter their cabin, we are met by a woman that we assume is the mother. Myack asks if Almigaq and Tuvartaq, the two brothers, are home. We find them sitting at a table in the cabin.

Myack introduces us to them and explains the purpose of our visit. Their mother says we are an answer to her prayers. She says her sons will be eager to learn. Both Almigaq and Tuvartaq agree that they desire to learn the subsistence ways of living a Yupik lifestyle. I ask if they each have a gun and ammunition. They say they have the guns that their father used and plenty of ammunition for both. They indicate that ducks and geese have returned for the summer.

"The slough is free of ice to allow us to kayak to the lakes where they are congregating," Almigaq says with excitement in his voice.

"Do you have a kayak that you can use?" I asked.

Almigaq says they have one tied up behind their smokehouse. I tell them we will return tomorrow morning to go duck hunting with them.

I tell Myack we should try to find a couple of kayaks that we may use while we teach the boys. She knows where we may find kayaks in the village and leads us to the people that have them. She says the people will gladly give their kayaks to have the much-needed food. I also ask her if she knows who may have a supply of wood for making a kayak. She said the man that was the village wood bender died during the sickness. His wood working shed still holds a large supply of wood. She is certain his wife would allow me to use the wood to build a new kayak for myself.

We stop at the cabins that Myack knows have kayaks. The women excitedly agree to offer their kayaks. We walked back to Myack's cabin with Kenruk and me carrying our newfound kayaks. They seem to be in good condition, so we will not need to make repairs to them. We are excited to be able to shoot some ducks and help the people obtain the much-needed food. During our walk, we discuss the time when the ice goes out so that we can begin catching salmon in the river.

The three of us return to Myack's cabin with our two kayaks. Anngaq is outside taking care of the dogs.

"You found kayaks!" he said in an excited voice.

He has the dogs tied to each doghouse that were left empty during the sickness that resulted in the killing of the dogs in the village. The dogs are happy with their new home and new grass lining each doghouse. Nayagaq is helping make dog soup with our supply of fish that we brought with us.

"The dogs deserve a good hot meal after all they have been through," she said.

I think how we depended upon these dogs to allow us to make this journey. I am so proud of these dogs, I think to myself.

It is a clear, sunny morning as Kenruk and I with our kayaks walk to the young men's cabin to guide us to the lakes for duck hunting. Almigaq and Tuvartaq set their kayak in the slough, followed by Kenruk and I in our two kayaks. We head down the slough in the direction of Ingriller, which is covered in sun and stands prominently above the flat tundra. We follow the young men as we go deeper into the tundra. We see several lakes to the west as we stop and anchor our kayaks.

The tundra is difficult walking and requires our tall mukluk boots to keep our feet dry. We see many ducks and geese swimming in the larger lake that is our destination. We find a group of willows that allows us to hide behind as we prepare our guns to shoot. I am reminded that this is very similar to shooting around the lake near our summer fish camp. I take my shot first, then Kenruk takes aim at the duck in his gun sights. We soon have two ducks. I am surprised the gun shot noise does not frighten the ducks, as they don't take flight. Kenruk and I quickly shot four more ducks.

I ask Almigaq and Tuvartaq if they want to shoot. They quickly agree to try their shooting skills. They know how to load their guns but aren't sure how to aim. I help Almigaq and Kenruk assist Tuvartaq with their aiming technique. They both shoot but miss. We tell them how to correct their mistakes. They again take aim, and they both make a kill. Eventually, our shooting has caused all the ducks to fly away. We walked to the lake and waded into the water to retrieve our catch. We are able to catch a dozen ducks from this lake.

We enter our kayaks and continue down the slough. The slough begins to narrow, which allows the ducks that sit on the water to become easier targets. Both Almigaq and Tuvartaq find their shooting skills as we continue deeper into the tundra. We continue to the end of the slough that forces us to turn around and head back to the village. We have a very successful harvest of ducks.

Our successful trip brings hope to the people. We have caught many ducks that can be shared with every person. We paddle the kayaks with a quick pace so we can quickly get the ducks to the people that need them most. We know how desperate the need for food has become, and we run to each cabin to share our catch. Every person is very thankful for the duck that is given to them. Kenruk and I return to Myack's cabin with news of our hunting trip. Myack greets us at her door with hugs and tears in her eyes.

"You both have made a huge impact on our village and possibly saved many lives," Myack adds after clearing the tears of joy from her eyes.

"Tomorrow we will catch rabbits from the tundra. I tell Myack we will catch enough food for the people to alleviate the famine." She is excited to hear our optimism that we can end the food crisis. Once the river is free of ice, we can begin fishing for salmon.

"I will use the interim time to build myself a new kayak," I say in my own excited voice.

With our short exchange, we enter her cabin and wonder what meal awaits us at the hands of Nayagaq. Myack's cabin was filled with so much joy that she was completely overwhelmed with our catch of ducks.

"How did Almigaq and Tuvartaq perform with their guns?" she asks.

Kenruk explains that in the beginning, we had to help them with their aim. They quickly learned the technique which corrected their aim. "They are now very proficient with their guns. I look forward to going with them to hunt rabbits," I said to Myack to further encourage her.

Nayagaq was happy to make bread for our evening meal. Myack said she hasn't made bread since before the sickness occurred. Anngaq helped Myack take the feathers off the two ducks I gave her. Nayagaq then cooked them for our evening meal. It was a very good meal of duck that we had not been able to eat since last fall before they migrated south.

After the meal is complete, Kenruk and I walk to the river to check on the ice conditions. We notice the ice has almost gone past. It is not completely ice-free as we had hoped. Before we return to our smokehouse, I stop by the carpenter shed that holds the wood for making a kayak. I entered the shed and was surprised to see a large amount of wood—more than enough to make a kayak. The shed has two stoves and two bending boxes that will make my work go twice as fast.

We walked to our smokehouse, and I am hopeful about building a new kayak. I look forward to applying what Pa taught me regarding his wood bending skills. As I go to sleep, my final thoughts are about our rabbit hunt tomorrow. I am hopeful that we can catch a lot of rabbits for the village women.

The next morning is a repeat of the one before with sunshine and warm weather. After our morning meal, Almigaq and Tuvartaq bring their kayak in anticipation of today's rabbit hunt. They are excited to go hunt rabbits on the tundra today. They explain where the good rabbit habitat is located as Almigaq remembers where his Pa went to hunt rabbits. He adds that it is also a good ptarmigan nesting area. We are encouraged that we will have a good hunt and leave our cabin and take the kayaks to the slough.

We head down the slough, but this time we take a slough to the left rather than go down the slough as we did yesterday. The tundra in this direction has more willows growing near the slough. I think Almigaq is correct to go this way. The area looks good for rabbit nesting within the willow groves.

We stop to look over the area that is covered with willow groves throughout. The tundra is wetter in this area as we are near the river. The brown rabbits are more difficult to see as they blend into the background of the tundra. We examine the willows and notice several rabbits sitting at the base of the willows. Almigaq and Tuvartaq take aim with their guns and kill the two rabbits. They have become very good with their guns. We look at other willows and see many rabbits that are sitting in the warm sun. We caught many rabbits during our hunt. The rabbit population is very numerous, just as it was back in Kagemuit. We load our rabbit catch in our kayaks and head back to the village.

The addition of rabbits to the people's diet is well received. As we stop at each cabin, the women are very happy to get our catch. They have been in need for so very long. They realize the extra food that we are providing makes the difference between life and starvation. The two young men and

Kenruk and I have become hero saviors for the village. The village women come by to express their gratitude for the food we have provided to them.

Now that the village has a supply of food, I can now focus my attention on building my kayak. I will need a good one by the time the salmon enter the river. I think I may have only about two weeks to build my kayak before the fishing season begins. I don't want to be late. The village needs fish as soon as the salmon enters the river. I watched Pa build many kayaks. Now it is my turn to place those skills that he showed me and taught me to work. My Pa was a great teacher. I hope I can be his best pupil as I build my kayak without his presence.

The next morning, Kenruk and I go to the carpenter shop and begin sizing and cutting the wood into the correct size and length. Kenruk will be a great help, as both of us will be able to work more in less time. With two fires and two bending boxes, I think we can build it much faster than it would take Pa doing it alone with only one fire and bending box. Each day we work to bend wood and assemble my kayak. The shop also has an adequate supply of seal skins and sewing supplies to make the covering of my kayak.

While Kenruk and I build the kayak, the young men go hunting on their own. Each day they hunt, they come back and report to me the success of their hunt. I am gaining confidence that Almigaq with Tuvartaq's help can feed the people. The people now look to the young men as the new leaders of the village. The young men are becoming important to the village not only to exist but to continue. My next task will be to teach them set net fishing.

During the time we wait for the salmon to arrive, we check the nets in the village for any needed repairs. This is another teaching moment for me to give Almigaq the opportunity to provide this essential talent for the village. We want all the nets to be ready once fishing begins. While we wait for the first salmon, the older women recite the elders' predictions of the arrival of fish. Myack tells me that the arrival of birds indicates the arrival of fish.

"If the birds come early, then the fish will arrive early. If the birds arrive in large groups, then the fish will arrive in large numbers," Myack recites the saying of previous elders of her village.

She also states that the elders could predict where the salmon will enter the river determined by the wind direction. "If the wind comes from the north and west, then the fish will enter the south mouth of the river. If the wind comes from the south, the fish will favor the north mouth of the river." Myack admits that without their elders, the village is without a clear direction of fishing success.

Each day we are busy with building the kayak and making net repairs. The final step of our kayak building is covering it with seal skin. Nayagaq helps with sewing the skins together and covers the kayak with them. She has learned skin sewing well from her Ma. She demonstrates those skills with a show of a job well done attitude. With the kayak covered in seal skin and treated with seal oil, it is now ready for fishing season.

Since the fish have not arrived yet, we decided to use our quiet time to gather eggs. The waterfowls are in egg-laying mode at this time of year. I want to try out my new kayak to check its handling on the water. Kenruk and I use my new kayak. Anngaq and Myack use Myack's kayak.

We head down the slough that leads to the tundra that is not covered in so many willows. It is more open with many lakes and small ponds. This is the area that should have numerous nests that are used by ducks, geese, and swans. We are not disappointed with the large number of nests. Each nest has many eggs, but we only take one or two from each. We want little birds to hatch, grow, and flourish so they will return next year. We filled our baskets and returned to the village.

As we always do with our harvest, we share the eggs with the villagers. Each person will have access to the protein provided by adding eggs to their diet. The entire village is no longer living in fear of having no food. It is now a vibrant community looking forward to the future it now has. There is joy, happiness, and a sense of hope that became contagious throughout the people. As many people praise what we did for the village, I just tell them we simply wanted to help.

The ice has left the river for over several days now, and we are considering setting our nets the next day. The local women tell me that a good place to set our net is on the flat island that is situated between the river and the sea. I go to sleep dreaming of a bountiful catch of salmon.

Chapter 18

The morning sun is hidden by clouds on the first day of fishing. The temperature is cooler than it has been since we arrived at Nunam Iqua. We are excited to try our hand at fishing so close to the ocean.

"I am experienced with fishing along the river, but I am not sure how my experience will work this close to the ocean," I said. I hope Almigaq and Tuvartaq will be able to guide us to the good fishing sites.

"They have helped their Pa fishing, but now they must do it alone without his help," Kenruk says.

We completed our morning meal, and Kenruk and I loaded the net, buoy, and anchor in my kayak. We place our kayaks in the water and paddle down to the two young men's cabin. Almigaq and Tuvartaq were loading their fishing gear into their kayak as we stopped to discuss our strategy. Almigaq says he remembers his Pa's fishing site on an island that is near the ocean. I agree that we will set our net at that site. Just as we prepare to set off down the slough, their Ma runs out with a bag and gives it to Almigaq. It is a lunch she has prepared for all of us. We thank her for her thoughtfulness as we continue down the slough to the river.

There is a large island that we go around to head downriver. We aren't in the river very long before we see another large island that sits at the end of the river. The river is very wide with submerged sandbars everywhere. I will have to learn how to read the water, as I seem to hit every sand bar in the river. Kenruk is having the same difficulty as I in navigating the river to avoid the sand bars. We will need to have Almigaq lead the way next time to help us avoid the sandbars. I signal to Almigaq to go ahead of me as I get out of my kayak to push off the sandbar that I am stuck upon.

Almigaq maneuvers his kayak toward the large island and finds a place to which he anchors. Kenruk and I land our kayaks beside his. It is a very large, flat island with no vegetation. I get an eerie feeling standing in a place where I look to the west and see nothing but water. I turned to look to the east and see only the river. Almigaq states that this is the island from which we will set our nets.

The clouds still exist, and the breeze from the ocean makes it very cool. Almigaq and Tuvartaq work to set one end of their net along the island and use their kayak to pull the net out into the river. When they get their net in the river, they drop the anchor with a beluga gut buoy floating on the water.

"The two young men are very proficient at net setting," I tell Kenruk.

"Yes, their Pa has taught them well," Kenruk adds.

They bring their kayak onto the beach to give us directions as to where we should position our net. Kenruk and I use my kayak to set our net where they indicate. As we stand on the island and watch our nets, we notice that our nets are the only ones in the river. Almigaq explains that by the time the salmon enter the river in large numbers, there will be many fish camps set upon the riverbank across from us.

"Where do the people come from who fish here?" I ask.

Tuvartaq answers to say that people from down the ocean coast come here to fish. He adds, "My Pa's ancestors came here to fish from down the coast." He further states that eventually his grandpa and grandma decided to move and settle in Nunam Iqua.

"It simply made more sense to them to live where the fishing occurs," Tuvartaq says. He also adds that this area has the best berry picking sites within easy distance.

"People from upriver come here to fish, especially those that live in Alarneq," Almigaq adds to the conversation.

I ask, "Where is Alarneq?"

Almigaq tells me that it is the next village upriver. "It is a settlement on the north side of the river," Almigaq adds more detail to its location. After Almigaq explains the village upriver, I think to myself that it may be a possible settlement site that I can consider or somewhere nearby.

I ask Almigaq why he has anchored his net farther up the island than I did. He began talking about tides. I have heard about tides but was not sure how they affect fishing. He answers that tides are created by the moon. The moon causes ocean water to rise and fall. They occur in regular cycles.

"I know that the tide is coming in, so that is why I positioned the net as I did," Almigaq explains. He further adds, "The water will rise during the next few hours and will raise the net as it does." He continues to explain that the water will eventually go back down when it reaches its highest point.

"This is why we set our nets when we did this morning—to take advantage of the rising tide," Tuvartaq adds. He says, "A rising tide will actually push the fish into the river."

I tell Kenruk that we have much to learn while we fish this river.

Almigaq says the land next to the river is home to a large nesting population of waterfowl. "I forgot to tell you to bring your guns so we can go hunt birds," he apologizes to us. While we wait to check our nets, we go across the river to the north and try to catch some birds. The north bank of the river is a wide open area of flat tundra without any willows. It is covered with numerous ponds and lakes. We see more ducks and geese than I can comprehend. They are everywhere, I tell myself. Almigaq and Tuvartaq use their guns to shoot many birds.

"The village people are still in need of food as they wait for the salmon to arrive," Almigaq says.

While they shoot birds, Kenruk and I hunt for eggs.

"I have not seen so many nests in one place," Kenruk says to me.

I agree and tell Kenruk that the people will eat well when we arrive back in the village. Even if we catch no fish this time, there will be plenty of food to bring back to the village. We gather our catch of birds and eggs and bring them to our kayaks. It is a short trip to the island where we decide to open the bag of food that their Ma has provided.

She filled it with smoked salmon and pilot crackers. It was just what we needed after a busy morning of setting the net and going hunting. As Almigaq promised, the water has risen, and the net is fully floating on the river. We can tell by looking at the net that no salmon has been caught.

"Obviously, we are early, as the salmon have not entered the river," Almigaq explains.

Tuvartaq adds, "They will come. We just need to be patient."

"We will come back tomorrow and check the nets," Almigaq says with optimism in his voice.

We may have no fish, but we bring birds and eggs back to the village as food. We let Almigaq lead us this time in his kayak to avoid the sandbars. As we paddle upriver, Kenruk and I agree that the young men understand fishing very well. They have learned what their Pa taught them. Over time, both will become valuable persons to the village. I believe they will become village elders as they grow in age and wisdom.

When we open the door to Myack's cabin, Nayagaq asks, "How many fish did you catch?"

I reply, "No fish, but we bring you a goose and five eggs."

"But I wanted salmon for the evening meal," she said with a touch of laughter in her voice.

I assured her that they will come when they decide to swim upriver to spawn. Myack gets the cookstove fire going to prepare the goose and have fried eggs for our evening meal.

Anngaq and I go out to the dog yard so I can check on the dogs. I ask Anngaq how the dogs are adjusting to their new home. He says they are eating and sleeping as if they were back home in Kagemuit. He did say that we are getting low on our dried fish supply. I tell him that the fish should arrive any day. Anngaq reminds me that we lost most of our dried fish that was stored in Pa's sled that went underwater during the river crossing.

As we walk back to the cabin, Anngaq stops and tells me that he likes Myack.

I reply, "She is a very intelligent person and a leader among the women in the village."

"You think it is alright for me to like her?" Anngaq asks as though he wants my older brother opinion.

I, without hesitation, respond, "Yes."

We continued our walk to Myack's cabin from the dog yard.

The aroma of cooked goose fills the cabin as we enter. We also smell fresh bread that Nayagaq had made to accompany the salmon that she was expecting. While we eat our fresh goose and fried eggs, Myack asks how the two young men have demonstrated their fishing skills. She says that their Pa was one of the best fishermen in the village.

I tell her, "It is obvious they have been taught by someone with a lot of experience."

"I certainly had problems navigating the sandbars in the river," I told her. "I needed Almigaq to lead the way to the fishing site," I said.

"Have other fish camps arrived?" Myack inquired.

I told her that we were the only ones setting a net, and no fish camps were seen.

The next morning, we meet Almigaq and Tuvartaq at their cabin. I have Almigaq lead the way again to their fishing site so I can avoid any sandbars. We can sense that no salmon have been caught in the nets, as the net floats are all riding high on the water. We turn our kayaks around and head back to the village. We repeat our efforts for the next few days without any salmon in our nets. We must be patient, I tell myself.

People begin arriving from upriver and down the ocean coast to set up their fish camps on the south bank of the river. After checking our nets, we stop and visit a few of the many fish camps. Almigaq and Tuvartaq recognize the people and introduce them to Kenruk and me. They indicate that the salmon should arrive any day. The riverbank that was devoid of anyone when we arrived from our journey is now becoming a tent city of fish camps.

Another morning dawns, and we repeat our kayaking routine. There are many nets in the water as people are setting their nets in anticipation of the beginning of fishing season. We approach our nets and notice that they have caught salmon. We are excited, as both of our nets have salmon. Kenruk and I draw the net across our kayak and pick the king salmon from the net and lay them into the bottom of our kayak. They are the largest fish I have ever handled. It is true that Kuigpak kings are the largest of any salmon in any river in the territory. Even Kenruk, as strong as he is, was having difficulty handling some of the fish. There were not many fish, but they did fill our kayak. Almigaq and Tuvartaq were also picking fish from their net.

"The kings have arrived!" was Almigaq's excited exclamation.

Chapter 19

We brought our first catch of salmon to the village. We have enough to share and give to each woman in the village. It is an exciting time to catch the first king salmon of the season. This is what everyone has been waiting for since the sickness had taken its toll on the people of Nunam Iqua. The women are now able to use their fish cutting tables and ulus again. Now the fishing season has begun. People can depend on a steady supply of food.

It became a daily ritual of checking the net. The number of king salmon increased with each passing day. On the river there were kayaks constantly coming from and going to people's nets. The tent city of fish camps were very busy processing fish.

All members of every family were busy with their job in cutting fish and drying them. Even the youngest family members were busy carrying fish parts to feed the dogs that were brought to fish camp. Since kings were also smoked, each smokehouse was busy with smoke fires. The entire area smelled of smoke from each smokehouse. It was exciting and heartwarming to see the happy faces of everyone. With the very long days of sunshine, the work at each camp went almost day and night. All the families wanted to process as many fish as possible to meet their needs for the coming winter.

In the village there was also fish cutting activity that kept everyone busy. The fish caught by Kenruk and me were shared with Myack and the rest of the women in the village. We tried to share the salmon equally with everyone.

I tried not to short any people of our king salmon catch. Some women could not cut fish, so Kenruk and I and my brother and sister helped cut fish. So many women lived without a husband and needed our extra support.

Every fish drying rack and smokehouse were beginning to fill with dried or smoked fish. Myack, Nayagaq, and Anngaq had a well-worked fish cutting routine to fill her drying rack and smokehouse. The dogs really enjoyed having an almost endless supply of fish parts during each meal. Anngaq continued to care for the dogs while Kenruk and I worked the fish nets.

There is a sense of renewed life within the village with the arrival of salmon. People are outside talking with each other and helping those in need of assistance. There is also an occasional group laughter as the women gather to share their fishing experience.

"The village has changed from dread to hope with the arrival of salmon," I tell Myack.

Myack agrees with my thoughts as she says, "You and your family and cousin have changed the very character of our village. You have brought so much hope where none existed before your arrival," she says.

Eventually the king salmon season comes to a close with the arrival of chum salmon. I know that chum season can become a very busy time as they come in greater numbers.

Even though the chum salmon are smaller and easier to handle, the greater volume of fish makes work continue day and night. Simply, the more fish, the more work required. Much of the chum salmon catch goes toward the dog teams. Since all the dogs were eliminated from the village, the chum catch eventually goes to feed people. Nunam Iqua should end up with a large supply of extra salmon going into the winter. The chums come in groups, and when a lull develops, it is time to rest.

I use this time to visit with the people that come from upriver. I stopped at a fish camp from the upriver village of Alarneq. The upriver country has been of interest to me as a possible site for me to settle. When I listen to these people, they speak of other rivers that flow into the ocean. The Alarneq villagers told me that there is a slough that connects their village with a portion of the river that flows into the ocean. At the end of that river is a large island that should be good for fishing. They also tell me that no one lives on this river. I ask if anyone fishes this river. They say they are not aware of anyone fishing there. They all agree that this area of the river is the best fishing location.

I also took advantage of another chum catch reduction to visit with people that came from areas down the coast. They came from a river that empties into the ocean. This river is much smaller than the Kuigpak and does not attract many salmon. It is a short river and does not provide the spawning grounds that salmon require. I ask how far this river is from the Kuigpak. They say it is a one-day journey by kayak. I consider what was just told to me, and I believe that may be the river where Pa and Ma fell through the ice. This may be the village that we decided to avoid during our trip north to the Kuigpak River after the accident.

I consider all the conversations I heard during my visits. I try to assimilate all this information into ideas that I can use to focus on my future and reflect on the past. I think that someday the people from the coast may find evidence regarding the loss of Pa and Ma. Maybe a portion of the sled may float to shore, and someone will find it as they walk along the seashore.

The conversations I had with the people living upriver encouraged me to consider that area as a possible settlement site. I am a river person, not an ocean dweller. The area of which they speak sounds like my open tundra type of living that I am searching for. It does not sound like anyone has settled there. It could be my very own settlement to afford me a fresh, new start to my life. I am encouraged by the prospects that may lay before me.

Chum season continues at a frantic pace. Kenruk and I must work at an almost nonstop pace to keep up with the chum catch. There will be significantly more fish than the village may need. I discuss this idea with Almigaq and Tuvartaq to get their opinion. They have been very busy fishing just like us. They also think we may be reaching the maximum catch of salmon that the village needs to carry it through the winter.

I think I should discuss this with Myack. They both agree that I should get her opinion. I talked to Myack and tell her about my concerns regarding the number of salmon the village needs. She has also noticed the large number of salmon that have been dried and smoked.

She states that she has been approached by a few unmarried men from the fish camps indicating that they are interested in the single women of their village. This will increase their population size, and that will require more fish. I agree that if that is true, we should continue fishing. Myack thinks we can stop catching chums in a couple of days. The fall chums will migrate next, and we can start fishing for them.

The Kuigpak fall chums are bigger and better quality than the dog chums that we are catching now. This I have been told by the women in the village. The fall chums that arrive early will be saved for people's consumption as they are the largest, brightest, and have not matured yet. The fall chums that arrive toward the end of the season are less desirable because they are more mature and not as good to eat. They will become food for the dogs. I agree with Myack's fishing strategy.

Within the two days that we still fish for chums, we catch many of them. We tell the women of our ending to fishing for chums. They agree that it is a wise decision. They say they always look forward to the fall chum season. The older women call them silvers because they are very bright silver in color. They add that the early fall chums are silver, but the later fall chums are more calico in color to reflect their more mature condition.

When the fall chums arrive, they do not disappoint me. They are very good quality and much larger than the summer chums we have been catching. They are not as numerous, so we are able to handle the catch each day. The women are very happy to be given our fall salmon catch. These fish are also smoked after they are dried, as their flavor is very sought after for meals. I am certain that by the time fishing season ends, the village will have an adequate supply of fish for the winter.

After our evening meal, while the days are still very pleasant, Anngaq wants to talk with me in private. We both walk to the dog yard as that is a quiet place where we can talk. Anngaq tells me that his interests in Myack have grown since we last talked. He expresses a desire to stay in the village with her rather than continue the journey with me. I tell him that he is making a good decision.

"Myack is a very good woman that is very respected by everyone in the village," I reassure him. I further add, "I respect your decision, and it is fine with me for you to stay with the one you love. Your happiness and contentment in your life is what is most important to you," I add.

"Is it alright for me to stay?" Anngaq asks.

"You have found your place in life, and it should be here in Nunam Iqua with Myack," I tell him as I approve of his decision.

"Thank you, brother," was Anngaq's reply.

During the next evening meal, Anngaq announces to everyone that he will be staying in Nunam Iqua with Myack. Myack comes to Anngaq and gives him a big hug and a kiss to confirm to everyone that she agrees. Nayagaq goes to Myack and gives her a hug to congratulate her for their decision.

The fall chum season comes to an end. The fish camps begin to disappear one by one as the people go back to their own village. Soon the south bank is empty of tents. It seems so deserted now. It was so full of life during fishing season. Some of the single men have taken up residence with the younger women that have lost their husbands during the sickness. It is becoming a real village once again. I can feel the new life that has transformed it from the seemingly lifeless one we entered a few months ago.

I ask Nayagaq what plans she has going forward from here. She says Myack has told her about a mission school located on a river east of here.

"It is called Akuluraq, and they provide education for orphaned children," she says with an excited voice.

"You don't want to marry any of the young men in this village?" I ask.

She responds, "Almigaq and Tuvartaq are very nice young men, but I don't want to live here. I am like you. I am a river girl. I just don't feel like I belong here by the ocean. I want to do something that will help others, especially the orphaned children," she says.

I reassure her, "I understand completely, Nayagaq. You were always one to help others in need. The orphaned children without parents need someone like you to care for them. It is your destiny to go to this place called Akuluraq."

Nayagaq asks, "When can you take me there?"

I reply, "I don't know the way to Akuluraq."

Nayagaq says, "Myack knows the way. She can explain it to you or guide us there."

That evening after our evening meal, Nayagaq and I meet with Myack to discuss the route to Akuluraq. She says she has been there several times and knows the way. I ask her if she would be willing to guide us there. She says she and Anngaq can lead us there in their kayak, and Nayagaq and I can follow.

"When can we go?" Nayagaq asks Myack.

"We can leave tomorrow morning if you want," was Myack's reply.

Nayagaq said without hesitation, "That would be wonderful!"

"It has been a while since I have been to the mission. It will be good to return and visit with the workers," Myack says excitedly.

After the morning meal, we prepare our kayaks for the journey. Nayagaq places all her personal belongings in a bag and takes them to my kayak. Kenruk follows us to the kayak and gives Nayagaq a farewell hug and wishes her well in her new life at the orphanage. We place our kayaks in the water, and I follow Myack as we go down the slough and then head east.

The journey takes most of the day as the slough makes many turns and switchbacks. This portion of the tundra has no willows. We can see forever from our kayak. The mountain we call Ingriller is always in sight because of the barren tundra to the south. Our kayaks cause many ducks to take flight ahead of us. If I only had my gun, I thought. After many hours of paddling, we see the large two-story buildings of the mission ahead.

It takes many more turns in the slough before we reach our destination. We dock our kayaks and begin walking to the large building we assume is the mission. We are met by women that we think are nuns. Myack recognizes the women and introduces us to them. They are happy to see Myack again. They ask what brings her to the mission. Myack tells them that Nayagaq wants to help at the orphanage. They are very excited that she wants to help with the work here. They say that because of the sickness, the work at the orphanage has been overwhelming. They can use more people like Nayagaq to assist with the children.

It is time for the evening meal, so they invite us to join them. We are all hungry, so we don't hesitate to accept their meal offering. As we enter the meal hall, we are met by a priest that appears to be the leader of the mission. The nun that we first met introduces Nayagaq to him with her intention to stay and help with the mission work.

"That is wonderful," he says. "We need more young women willing to help with our work," he says to Nayagaq.

Nayagaq replies, "I am happy to help with the work that is being done here."

As we eat our evening meal, the priest explains the history of the mission. He tells us that the mission was first located on the Kanelik River to the north. That site did not work well because the land was too low and subject to flooding. It was then moved here on the Akuluraq River because it is much higher ground. This river is larger and deeper to accommodate the barges that bring their supplies. They maintain large gardens to grow much of their vegetables. They had to bring in the soil to create a suitable garden site.

He further explains that they are providing for the needs of many children that have been orphaned by the pandemic. "We need everybody to help us with the mission work. We also provide education for the children."

He also informs us that the territory will be introducing reindeer herding on the nearby tundra. The territory law requires that only native Eskimos will be allowed to oversee the herds. The reindeer will provide much-needed meat and hides for the local area. It should be an economic boost to the local villages. He thinks the program should begin in the near future.

By the time he finishes, it gets dark, and he suggests we stay for the night in the dormitories. I am overwhelmed by the sleeping rooms that we are provided with. I have never slept in such luxury. Anngaq and I sleep in the boy's dormitory, and Nayagaq and Myack sleep in the girl's dormitory.

In the morning, we are treated to a very nice morning meal of bacon, eggs, and pancakes. I haven't eaten a morning meal like this since Nuliaq prepared one while we stayed at Tagneq's store in Mamimuit. After the meal, we prepare to leave and say goodbye to Nayagaq. She walks with us down to our kayaks. She gives Myack a hug and thanks her for the hospitality she showed to her at her cabin. She gives a brotherly hug to Anngaq and wishes him the best as he lives with Myack.

Nayagaq walks over to me with tears in her eyes and gives me a long emotional hug. With tears still in her eyes, she says, "I will miss you most, Qataruaq. You have been a wonderful big brother to me."

It was just as emotional to me as I tell her, "I will forever miss you. We have been through so much together."

We released our hug, and I walked toward my kayak. As I depart and paddle away, I look back to see Nayagaq waving to me. I raise my paddle toward her in a display that I am proud that she is my sister. It takes us most of the day to journey back to the village. Kenruk is standing on the bank of the slough to welcome us home.

I told Kenruk that I plan to go upriver in search of a place to settle. I ask him, "What are your plans, Kenruk?"

He replies, "Wherever you go, I want to go. We have gone this far together. I may as well complete this journey with you."

I tell him, "I could use a travel partner."

We shake hands to confirm our relationship.

Kenruk says that the village is planning a potlatch tomorrow evening to honor our efforts to save the village. "I guess we have to stay one more day," I tell Kenruk.

The next day we spent our time preparing for our journey upriver. Kenruk can have the kayak as his own, says the woman that we borrowed it from. We load the fishing gear in Kenruk's kayak. I load the winter trapping gear in my kayak. I tell Kenruk that we have everything that we need to make camp except for a tent. Kenruk tells me, "We will have to rough it for a while."

Myack finds us to say that the potlatch in our honor is to start as soon as we make our way to the qasgiq. "We better not keep them waiting," was my reply. As we enter the qasgiq, we are greeted by the entire village people. The women had brought the best of their foods to treat us. There was so much food before us to eat. The women give us a portion of their prepared food. We thanked each lady for the food they were serving to us.

After everyone had finished their meal, we were told to take a place near the fire pit. The women performed an Eskimo dance that they had prepared just for us. Almigaq and Tuvartaq beat the drums as the women danced. I was very impressed with their dance motions. These women have come a long way since the time when we first arrived at their village. They were on the edge of starvation back then, and now we watch them dance with so much excitement, joy, and energy.

After the dance was completed, Myack comes forward and hands me a new white wall tent. "It has never been used, and our people want you to have it as you make your new home," she says, and everyone stands in recognition. Kenruk and I stand to receive this wonderful gift from the village. I tell them that we had everything to set up camp except for a tent.

"This is a gift we will cherish and remember all of you for the rest of our lives," Kenruk and I speak in unison.

Another woman comes forward and speaks, "We owe you both our very lives for providing the much-needed food. You have demonstrated an example of friendship that we will remember forever. We wish you good fortune in your every endeavor." She hands us two bags and continues to speak, "You gave us much food in our time of need. Please accept these bags of dried and smoked fish as our way of saying thank you."

I say "quyana" in reply. Kenruk gives her a hug.

At the close of the potlatch, we walk back with our tent and two bags of fish to Myack's cabin. Kenruk and I retire in the smokehouse for the final time. I tell Kenruk, "It has been a wonderful day." Kenruk agrees that it has been a wonderful day.

The morning brings bright sunshine and warm temperatures. "It will be a great day for kayaking," I tell Kenruk. Myack invites us for the morning meal at her cabin. Everyone has much to talk about as we remind ourselves about how far we have come and the journey ahead. Anngaq adds his stories of the journey from Kagemuit. The three of us reminisce about all that happened to us during the trip north. We remember the great excitement we felt when we saw the big river. Our talk became subdued as we remembered the tragedy at the river crossing with the loss of Ma and Pa and the dogs.

Kenruk and I prepare to leave the cabin with hugs from both Myack and Anngaq. I tell them that we should be able to return for a visit sometime during the winter. "I hope to come back during the winter and pick up my sled and dog team," I tell Anngaq. Kenruk and I walk down to our loaded kayaks and take our seat in the kayak and shove off and head toward the river.

Chapter 20

We head down the slough with Anngaq and Myack waving from the shore. We waved our goodbyes to them. As we continue past the village, we are waved goodbye to by everybody that has come out of their cabins to send us on our way. We raise our paddle to salute the thankful attitude they had demonstrated to us.

We enter the Kuigpak River and head north. The river is very wide as we enter. We have calm water to make our paddling against the current not so difficult. We aim our kayak toward the north bank as our next destination is the village of Alarneq. I am overwhelmed by the size of this river. It is a new experience to navigate one this large. The river current is not as strong as I expected, likely because we are close to the ocean. I remember Almigaq talking about the tides. Maybe the tide is coming in, and that makes the current not as fast.

I always think it takes forever to paddle upriver. I am not as patient as I should be. I just need to remind myself that the steady paddle will get me to my destination. To my hopefulness, we eventually see the river seem to split. We continue to stay on the north bank and enter the channel. The island that splits the river leads us to a slough that brings us away from the main river.

We continue to follow this slough just like the people at fish camp told us. As they promised, it leads to a group of cabins on the south side of the slough. Our approach to the village brings the children to the shore to greet us as we beach our kayaks. They seem puzzled by our approach. They likely don't get many people in kayaks visiting their village. The children's excitement brings the parents to the shore to welcome us upon our arrival.

They recognize us from the fish camp visits that we made while fishing. They are happy to see us. The elder of the village appears among the group and invites us to his cabin for coffee.

"That sounds good to have a cup of coffee after our time kayaking," I tell him.

He leads us to his cabin and invites us inside. He introduces himself as Paluqtaq and his wife as Iligvak. I introduce myself as Qataruaq and my cousin Kenruk. Paluqtaq tells us that his village is called Alarneq, which means "wrong way" in the Yupik language. I tell him that it is a good name, as the island splits the river and it is difficult to know which way to follow. He gives us numerous examples of where people ended up at his village in their attempt to go upriver. This happened so often that they decided to name it "wrong way," or Alarneq in their language.

He explains that the village was settled by a Yupik shaman named Anguksuar and his family. No one knows why he settled here.

"Maybe he was heading up the river and took the wrong channel and ended up here," Paluqtaq said with laughter in his voice.

I ask him how the fishing season went for the villagers. He says it was a good fishing season. Everyone has a full smokehouse going into the winter. He states that people will be leaving to go berry picking in a few weeks. I asked him where they go to pick berries.

"The tundra south of Nunam Iqua is where we go," is his answer. He adds that the salmonberries are very large in that area.

"The blueberries are also very large and plentiful near there," his wife, Iligvak, adds. She further adds, "The blueberries we pick there make very tasty akutaq."

I also ask about the trapping opportunities near Alarneq. "As you can see, we only have barren tundra near our village, so trapping is not possible here. We must go north to find the willows available that provide us with better trapping conditions. The area near the river you are going offers much better trapping opportunities," Paluqtaq says. Paluqtaq says that they are seeing a few young willows beginning to grow in their area. The future may allow for trapping if they continue to grow and flourish.

"That gives me considerable encouragement as I travel to the river you call Kuiguk. I should be able to trap and snare with some success," I reply to Paluqtaq.

Kenruk seems to take the information as helpful and hopeful for good trapping. It is getting late, so Paluqtaq offers their qasgiq for us to use for the night. We excitedly accepted his offer. Kenruk and I walk to our kayak to gather our blankets.

As we pick up our belongings, we notice a family of otters swimming near our kayaks.

"It looks like this family of otters are protecting our kayaks," I tell Kenruk.

The days are getting shorter as the sun begins to set as we enter the qasgiq. Once we lay out our blankets for the night, we wonder what tomorrow will bring.

This is the final day of our long journey. Where will it lead us? What will it look like? Will we recognize it when we find it? Will we be happy when we finally set foot on our next adventure in our life? So many questions with no known answers as I lay down to sleep.

The final day of our journey begins with a beautiful sky with comfortable temperatures for paddling the kayak. Paluqtaq stops by the qasgiq to invite us for a morning meal before we depart. We are happy about the invitation and walk to his cabin. Iligvak is busy boiling water and preparing fish soup.

"I want you to have a hearty meal before you depart," she says.

Labrador tea is a good addition to the soup to warm us before we depart.

Paluqtaq provides us with directions to get us to the Kuiguk River by following the slough to the west. He tells us not to take the first slough to the right as it is a dead-end slough in the tundra.

"You will want to take the second slough to the right. If you take the slough to the left that heads west, you will end up at the ocean coast. The slough to the right will take you north, then east. This slough has many twists and turns. Stay straight with the main channel, and it will enter into the Kuiguk River near an island in the middle. Go to the right with the upriver current, and your destination is wherever you want to settle," Paluqtaq says with his experience of the area.

"These are good directions so that we should be able to find our way," I tell him.

"Bring your guns, as you will see many ducks on the water in the slough for shooting," Paluqtaq adds.

"We thank you for the detailed route directions you have given us," Kenruk and I reply.

We thank Iligvak for the delicious morning meal she provided. As we leave the cabin, she gives us a bag of dried fish for our trip.

"You need to eat good while you paddle your kayaks," she says in that motherly tone.

We walk to our kayaks and begin our journey up the slough.

We leave the village quietly and follow Paluqtaq's advice and paddle past the first slough to the right. We take the next slough on the right that heads north and then turn east. We stop to load our guns as it does look like good duck country that we are approaching. It would be good to catch some ducks on the way. This section of our journey is on tundra that has no willow vegetation at all. This slough has many turns. Around each turn we see ducks. Our approach makes most of the ducks take flight and are too far away for a good shot. There are some ducks that stay on the water and give us a good target as food for an upcoming meal. We catch enough ducks to satisfy our needs, and then we simply paddle without being distracted by ducks.

We have otters pay us a visit as we pass by their dens. I don't think they like us trespassing in their territory. They do break up the monotony of our journey. If we don't see ducks on the water, then we see them fly overhead.

"This area sure has a lot of waterfowl," Kenruk says from his kayak following me.

The farther we continue, we begin to see willows on the tundra. I believe this means that the river may be nearby. The willows become numerous and taller, until the slough opens into a river with an island in the middle. It appears just as Paluqtaq described it to us. We enter the river and turn right to paddle upriver.

It is a river of significant size. I think it should be a good river for salmon fishing. Kenruk brings his kayak up to mine, and we discuss the good qualities of this area, and our optimism grows with each stroke of our paddle. Shortly after we talked between our kayaks, we are greeted by a seal that is enjoying the river.

"This area is looking better all the time," I tell Kenruk.

The seal brings his head above water to look at us and then submerges. It does this hide-and-seek routine several times until it submerges and heads down the river.

We continue paddling upriver as we see an island in the distance. We come closer to it and decide to take the left channel to go around it. It is a small island with only grass and no willows. Once we go past the island, we notice a white wall tent on the bank of the river. The tent is set up next to a slough.

There are people here, as we see a kayak next to the tent.

"It looks like they have arrived just a short time ago," I say to Kenruk.

"It does look like they have arrived recently," Kenruk says.

We see two people coming from the tent as we beach our kayaks.

We step out of our kayaks upon the hard, water-soaked beach and walk toward the two people standing near their tent. They seem as surprised to see us as we are of seeing them.

I approach the man and give him my greeting.

"Waqaa. I am Qataruaq, son of Unozroak, a Yupik, from the village of Kagemuit on the Kusquqvak River, and this is my cousin Kenruk," I tell him in my most polite tone.

The man replies, "Waqaa."

He says, "I am Kaviaq, and this is my wife Kelaaseq."

Then he continues his greeting, "Welcome to Imangaq—where the black fish swim."

Notes to the Reader

After I wrote my first book, *Molly Hootch, I Remember When*, I received additional information regarding my grandpa, Charlie Hootch.

He was born and raised in Kagemuit (now an abandoned village) on the Kuskokwim River upriver from Bethel, Alaska. He, his parents, sister, brother, and a cousin were forced to flee when the Spanish Flu of 1918 devastated his village. They spent six months traveling from Kagemuit to Emmonak on the Kwiguk Pass of the Yukon River. This is all that is known of my grandpa's life before settling in what is now Emmonak, Alaska.

It was a story that needed to be told as a remembrance of how the ancestry of the Hootch family originated in this Yukon village. Since so little is known of Grandpa's life before Emmonak, I took the liberty to retell his life in the form of a historical fiction account. My story would represent the life of grandpa as he lived a traditional Yupik life of subsistence along the Kuskokwim River and the journey to Emmonak.

My research, as told to me, rendered the Eskimo names of my grandpa as Qataruaq. His parents' Eskimo names were Unozroak and Arnack. No Eskimo names are known about his sister, brother, and cousin, so I took the liberty to give them fictional Eskimo names.

Anngaq, his brother, also known as Mike Hootch, married an older woman from Nunam Iqua named Myack. His sister, Nayagaq, did not want to marry and decided to go to Akulurak, where she lived for the rest of her life. His cousin, also known as Jimmy (Shotgun), continued the journey to Emmonak with grandpa.

All other people mentioned are fictional names that I gave them. All villages along the Kuskokwim River, other than Kagemuit, were given fictional Yupik names to add realism to the story. Waterways along the Kuskokwim River were given fictional Yupik names. I used the Yupik names for the rivers that were mentioned. The villages visited during the six-month journey were given their original Yupik place names.

According to historical records and my conversations, Nunam Iqua suffered greatly during the Spanish Flu. My grandpa and his cousin were able to use their subsistence skills to help the village recover from the devastating effects of the pandemic.

Imangaq, Yupik for "black fish," is the original name for Emmonak, Alaska, the final home of my grandpa, Charlie Hootch.

www.ingramcontent.com/pod-product-compliance
Lightning Source LLC
Chambersburg PA
CBHW070803100426
42742CB00012B/2230